THE ROYAL ALBERT HALL

Also by John Richard Thackrah

THE RIVER TWEED
THE UNIVERSITY AND COLLEGES OF OXFORD

THE ROYAL ALBERT HALL

by

JOHN RICHARD THACKRAH

TERENCE DALTON LIMITED
LAVENHAM . SUFFOLK
1983

Published by
TERENCE DALTON LIMITED

ISBN 0 86138 012 6

Text photoset in 11/12pt. Garamond

Printed in Great Britain at
The Lavenham Press Limited, Lavenham, Suffolk

©John Richard Thackrah 1983

Contents

Index of Illustrations

Acknowledgements

WITHOUT the help and co-operation of a considerable number of people this book could not have been written, and my grateful thanks are due to them all in greater or lesser degree.

In the first place it would have been impossible even to make a start without the blessing and encouragement of the Council and staff of the Royal Albert Hall. My thanks are due to the Council for permission to have unfettered access to the archives of the Hall and the valuable assistance of Marion Herrod, the Secretary and Lettings Manager, who bore the burden I put upon her with commendable charm and fortitude. Anthony J. Charlton, the General Manager, Alan Carter, Backstage Manager, and A. Beaver, Artistes' Door Attendant, also gave me considerable help, as did several other members of staff in their own particular spheres of activity.

H. J. Sice, joint Superintendent of the Corps of Honorary Stewards, provided important information about the organisation for which he shares overall responsibility.

To Sir Robin Mackworth-Young, Keeper of the Royal Archives at Windsor Castle, and Jane Langton, the Registrar, my thanks are due respectively for permission to use appropriate material from the archives and for providing the relevant extracts from an enormous number of books, documents and manuscripts.

Miss J. Coburn, Head Archivist of the Greater London Council, and C. Anthony H. James, Secretary of the Royal Commission of the Exhibition of 1851, also provided valued information for the early chapters of the book.

Thanks are due to James Cocker and Sons Limited for permission to use their reproduction of the Royal Albert Hall rose for the back of the dust jacket and to the following for permission to use their photographs, which are acknowledged individually where they have been reproduced; the Council of the Royal Albert Hall, C. Christodoulou, Radio Times Hulton Picture Library, The Scouts Association, J. D. Sharp, M. A. J. Stirling, Studio Cole Limited, and Josiah Wedgwood and Sons Limited.

Terence Dalton and the late Mrs June Dalton, John Venmore-Rowland and Robert Malster of my publishers also deserve thanks for their assistance and guidance during the course of production.

Last but by no means least I wish to thank my parents for their advice and encouragement, and assistance in research; above all for the typing and checking of the manuscript and proofs.

JOHN RICHARD THACKRAH

Thornton Dale,
North Yorkshire,
1983

Overleaf
Queen Elizabeth II looking at exhibits in a special exhibition illustrating the history of the Royal Albert Hall after lunching with the Council on 30th October 1974.

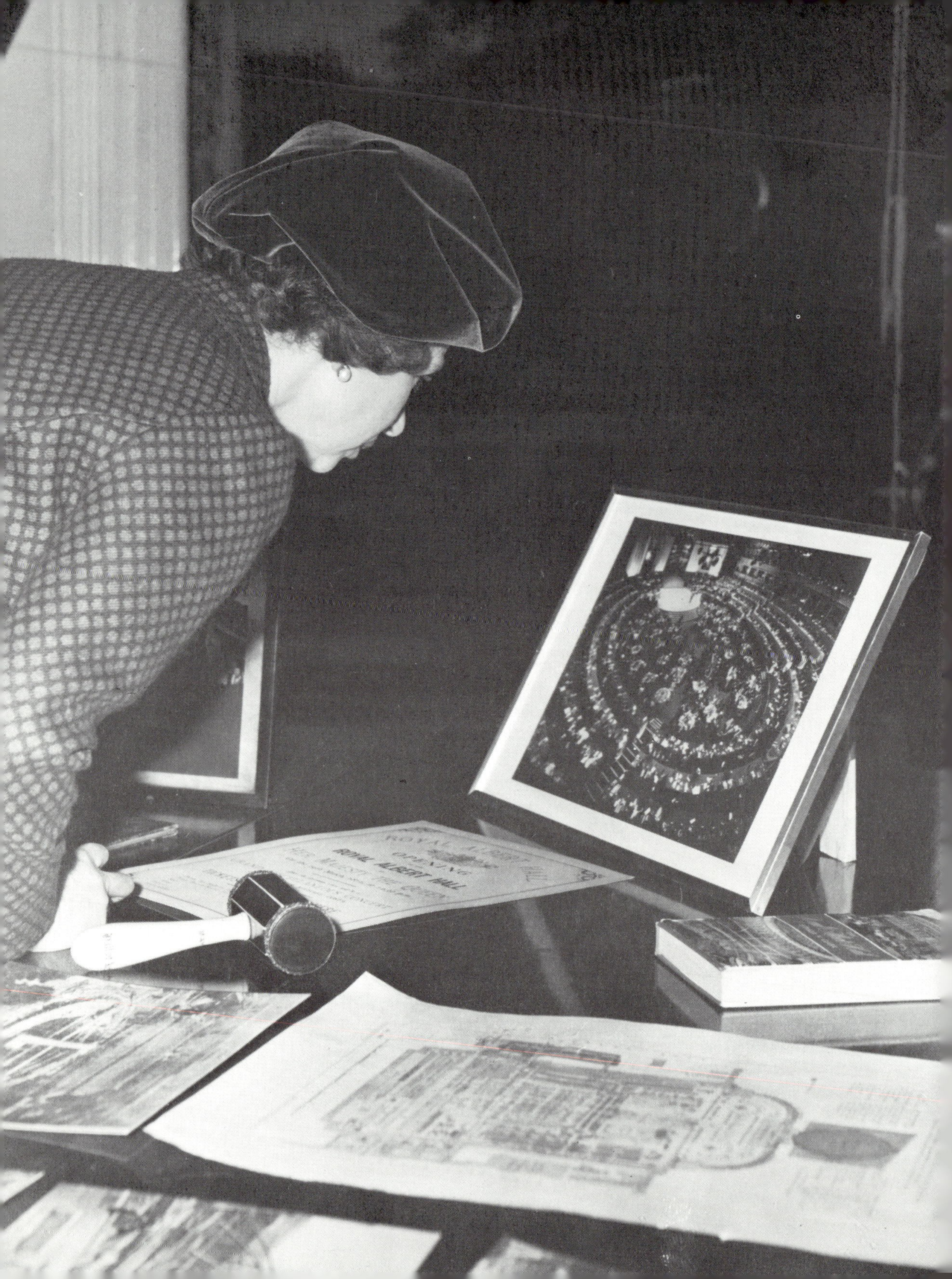
OPENING
ROYAL ALBERT HALL

CHAPTER ONE

In the Beginning

ON 14 December 1861 Prince Albert of Saxe-Coburg-Gotha, cousin and Consort of Queen Victoria, died of typhoid fever at Windsor Castle at the age of 42. This melancholy event in the Queen's long life, an event with which she was never fully able to come to terms, led to a development which Albert would have heartily endorsed and been proud to have as a lasting memorial to his services in the promotion of the arts and sciences in his adoptive country. A memorial happily still with us after a hundred years and still faithfully carrying out the duties entrusted to it by the vision of its founding fathers and several Acts of Parliament; even though those duties have been stretched to include events which could hardly be classified as either artistic or scientific unless granted the elasticity of improbable licence.

Over twelve years were to pass after the Prince's death before the great Colosseum-like structure of the Royal Albert Hall finally dominated the landscape of South Kensington, but the seeds of its birth had been sown long before the Prince's untimely death. His marriage to the Queen lasted 21 years and almost from the start she relied heavily on his advice and guidance since only a year after the pomp and circumstance of the wedding her wise and faithful counsellor, Lord Melbourne, resigned and Sir Robert Peel became Prime Minister, a move very much for the worse so far as she was concerned. However, this disaster, occurring so early in her reign, was soon to a large extent mitigated by the loyalty and counsel given to her by her husband. The Great Exhibition of 1851, held under his Presidency in Hyde Park, was an enormous success and achieved a profit of £186,436.

Albert had presided over an Exhibition Committee of Royal Commissioners who collectively could take much pride in their administrative and organisational drive which had done so much to promote British interests on an international scale. Now they were to go a stage further by purchasing in 1852 an estate in South Kensington as a site for Arts and Science Departments dealing with industrial education. £150,000 of the profit from the Great Exhibition was added to a Government grant of £177,500 to make up the purchase price, a bargain if ever there was one when the scene is surveyed today—a large rectangle bounded by Kensington Gore, Cromwell Road, Exhibition Road and Queen's Gate, crammed with buildings of great artistic and scientific import just as originally hoped for and conceived. Arguments and plans were bandied about and there was much heart searching, again with Albert playing a leading role. In his lifetime little of consequence developed but in all the proposals discussed a great hall was an essential feature.

Unfortunately the death of the Prince Consort brought proceedings to an abrupt halt and three and a half years were to elapse before a reaffirmation of interest manifested itself in a meeting at Marlborough House on 6 July 1865. This was no ordinary meeting because apart from being presided over by the Prince of Wales, later Edward VII, it was attended by no fewer than 70 lords and commoners. It was a gathering of highly influential persons, among them being the Prince's brother, George, Duke of Cambridge, five other Dukes, Devonshire, Rutland, St. Albans, Sutherland and Wellington, two Marquises, Lansdowne and Salisbury, seven earls, two viscounts and the Bishops of Bath and Wells, Winchester and Worcester. The purpose of the meeting was to promote "The erection of a Great Central Hall, the want of which for various purposes connected with Science and Art has been long felt." A Provisional Committee was duly appointed under the Chairmanship of the Prince of Wales and with Lieut. Col. Henry Young Darracott Scott, R.E., as Secretary. The latter's appointment had far reaching consequences and members of the Committee were unequivocally granted "Full powers to consider and adopt such measures as might appear to them calculated to carry into effect the proposed undertaking." It was decided that the Hall should be controlled by a Governing Body acting under authority of a Royal Charter and that its erection should be in memory of the Prince Consort. It was however nearly two years before the Royal Charter was granted on 8th April 1867.

The Charter established "The Corporation of the Hall of Arts and Sciences" naming the Members as Albert Edward, Prince of Wales, K.G. (Chairman); Alfred Ernest Albert, Duke of Edinburgh, K.G.; Edward Geoffrey, Earl of Derby, K.G.; Granville George, Earl Granville, K.G.; Lieutenant-General the Hon. Charles Grey; the Right Hon. Robert Lowe, M.P.; the Right Hon. Henry Austin Bruce, M.P.; Henry Cole, C.B.; Edgar Alfred Bowring, C. B.; Thomas Baring and Henry Thring. These same men, with the addition of John Fowler and under the Presidency of the Prince of Wales, were to constitute a Provisional Committee to act as the Corporation's governing body, supported by an Executive Committee consisting of the Duke of Edinburgh, Grey, Bruce, Cole, Bowring and Thring. Apart from the building and maintenance of the edifice the Corporation was empowered to utilise the Hall for:-

(a) Congresses, both National and International, for purposes of Science and Art.
(b) Performances of Music, including performances on the Organ.
(c) The Distribution of Prizes by Public Bodies and Societies.

(d) Conversaziones of Societies established for the promotion of Science and Art.
(e) Agricultural, Horticultural and the like Exhibitions.
(f) National and International Exhibitions of Works of Art and Industry, including Industrial Exhibitions by the Artizan Classes.
(g) Exhibitions of Pictures, Sculpture and other objects of artistic or scientific interest.
(h) Generally any other purposes connected with Science and Art.

The Supplemental Charter of 1887 extended these permitted usages by allowing the Council to:-

(a) Let the Hall aforesaid for any of the purposes hereinbefore authorised;
(b) Arrange with individual Members of the Corporation for the exchange, purchase, renting or temporary use of their boxes or seats.

These objectives stuck faithfully and firmly to the intentions not only of Prince Albert but also to those of the Commissioners for the Exhibition of 1851 and were subsequently to lead to considerable concern and disputation as to what was and was not either artistic or scientific. The Charter also made provision for the substitution, not later than the end of a year after the Hall's opening, of the Provisional Committee by an Elective Council and it is such a body which runs the Hall today.

Those specifically mentioned in the Charter had subscribed towards the funds for the erection of the Hall but there were many others and all were declared to be Members of the Corporation. There were three categories of membership—those donating £1,000, those giving £500 and those subscribing £100. In return for these donations the members respectively were entitled to:-

(a) A private box on the first tier of the Hall, containing ten seats,
(b) A private box on the second tier of the Hall, containing five seats,
(c) A seat in the amphitheatre of the Hall.

Alternatively a subscriber of £1,000 was entitled to two private boxes on the second tier and all subscribers of either £1,000 or £500 could take an equivalent number of seats in the amphitheatre in lieu of a box. Provision was also made for bodies Corporate to subscribe for seats and for Members to transfer their rights and obligations in respect of seats to another, either Member or otherwise, and in the event of bankruptcy, marriage or death; also their interest was to be regarded as personal estate rather than real estate.

Just over a fortnight before the granting of the Charter the Royal Commissioners on 25th March 1867 granted a 999 year lease of a site in Kensington Gore at a rental of one shilling (5p) per annum. The lease was conditional upon the public contracting not later than 1st May 1867 to invest sufficient funds to ensure completion of the building. The grant of the site was estimated to be worth some £50,000-£60,000 so the Corporation got off to a fine start so far as finances were concerned and the prestigious position that the future hall would occupy.

Amongst the first subscribers were the Queen and the Prince of Wales. Her Majesty chose two Grand Tier Boxes which now form the present Royal Box and the Prince selected one on the same tier but on the opposite side. Altogether 1,200 seats were disposed of by the time of the opening ceremony.

Prince Albert of Saxe-Coburg-Gotha, the Prince Consort.

The first plans for a hall were made by a curious and unlikely character, Professor Semper, who had been engaged by the King of Saxony to design the Dresden Theatre. Nothing came of Semper's efforts. Henry Cole was born in Bath in 1808 and at the age of fourteen joined the Civil Service. The destruction of the House of Commons by fire in 1834, at which calamity he busied himself with salvaging the public records, gave him the opportunity of initiating the Public Records Office from the documents that were saved and ultimately achieving the status of Assistant Keeper. He was a man of considerable versatility and amongst his achievements were the design of a tea service for which he was awarded the Silver Medal of the Society of Arts; guides to some of the capital's buildings including Hampton Court and the National Gallery; work in connection with the promotion of the Great Exhibition and a standard railway gauge. He also supported Rowland Hill's efforts towards a properly organised postal service.

Whilst walking home through the streets of London, on 19th February 1858 the two friends, Cole and Wentworth Dilke, a Commissioner for the 1851 Exhibition, discussed the possibility of holding yet another Great Exhibition in 1861 to display the nation's progress in a decade of achievement. It would appear that their only point of difference was in the form it should take, Dilke emphasising the priority of industry and Cole declaring that precedence should be given to the Fine Arts and music. To accommodate the performance of the latter nothing less than a magnificent new hall would be required. From such an innocuous beginning did the 1862 Exhibition stem. Cole soon used his influence to obtain the backing of Prince Albert and then went on a holiday tour of Europe. In the South of France he visited the Roman sites and immediately thought of his dream hall in terms of the Colosseum styles he encountered on his travels, even to the extent of committing his ideas to paper, albeit in somewhat crude form. Cole, in his impatience, sent his sketches by post back to London, to a friend who shared his enthusiasm and had considerable experience in the designing of buildings.

Francis Fowke, a Captain in the Royal Engineers, already had certain design achievements to his credit before getting involved with Cole's grandiose scheme; these included art galleries, barracks and libraries, a somewhat curious amalgam for a man with a military background. However, this was not all by any means, because Fowke was a man of many parts particularly in the line of inventions. Diversity would appear to have been a key-note to his activities which ranged from such things as a folding camera; a collapsible bath that could be carried under an arm and was euphemistically credited with being suitable for officers and gentlemen no less; and an umbrella which doubled up as a walking stick. On the military side his attentions were turned to a collapsible pontoon; a portable fire-engine and a specialist type of rifle-bullet. Cole's holiday impressions and Fowke's imaginative ideas were the springboard of the building to be seen today.

It was soon realised that the size of the proposed hall—it was to accommodate some 30,000 people—was much too ambitious for the finance likely to be available and in any case the plans for the 1861 Exhibition had to be postponed until a year later due to the Franco-Austrian War. So the ideas for a grandiose hall were put on ice though obviously with some regret and not only on the part of Cole for the Lord President of the Council, Earl Granville said to Lord Canning "We have been obliged to our great regret to excise a great Hall, which would have been the eighth wonder of the world." The regret expressed by Granville was almost certainly also in Prince Albert's mind when he opened the Horticultural Society's Gardens only a few months before his death. In his speech he expressed a wish "That it will, at no distant day, form the inner court of a vast quadrangle of public buildings, rendered easily accessible by the broad roads which will surround them; buildings where Science and Art may find space for development, with that air and light which are elsewhere well-nigh vanished from the metropolis.'' These were indeed prophetic words and, though not quite in the context which the Prince Consort envisaged, the array of public buildings and the broad roads of accessibility certainly came to pass and if he could return today there is little doubt that he would be immensely gratified. As it was his untimely death later in the year was, harnessed to Cole's driving enthusiasm, to prove the catalyst that brought the project to triumphant fruition.

The Prince's demise immediately brought demands for a memorial to him and eventually a group of seven architects drew up proposals to implement a

The Prince of Wales.

The Duke of Edinburgh.

suggestion by the Committee of Advice which had been appointed by the Queen for the purpose. The Committee comprised the Earls of Clarendon and Derby, the Lord Mayor of London, William Cubitt and the President of the Royal Academy, Sir Charles Eastlake. The brief to architects was that not only should there be a personal memorial but also a hall which would accomplish a desire held for so long by Albert in his lifetime. Messrs. Donaldson, Hardwick, Rennithorne, Scott, Smirke, Tite and Wyatt, all eminent members of the Royal Institute of British Architects, recommended in their report what was to transpire as the Albert Memorial standing in Kensington Gardens opposite the site of Albert's great Hall. Nine architects were invited to submit designs for the dual enterprise and the commission was given to George Gilbert Scott. Alas for the

Hall; there were financial problems since the public appeal to Albert's memory had only raised £60,000 to which the government added a further £50,000. As the Memorial alone was estimated to cost about £100,000 the combined efforts of public and government would only just cover the expenditure with little left over to put towards the estimated quarter of a million pounds required for the Hall. The result was once again the inevitable shelving of the Hall project though the Memorial proposal was approved and the scheme put in motion on 13th May 1864 and officially opened on 3rd July 1872.

Once again the indefatigable Cole set to work to overcome the difficulties. Towards the end of 1863 he revived his and Fowke's ideas for a concert hall, and issued a prospectus, only this time modifying the proposed capacity of the building from a highly improbable 30,000 to a more modest and practical 12,000. His scheme for financing the venture, estimated at £200,000, was basically similar to that which was eventually adopted with 500 individuals subscribing £100 each for perpetual admission and another 500 subscribing £50 for life admission. Additionally subscriptions were asked of £1,000 for the use of the Hall for one day annually in perpetuity, £1,750 for two days, £2,250 for three days and £500 for each day above three. Unhappily for Cole his ideas for financing the project were received with little enthusiasm and once again the proposals for the Hall appeared to be in serious jeopardy. A year was to pass with mounting frustration for Cole until he had the comparatively simple brainwave of requesting the Prince of Wales to become President of the Committee considering the project which had been virtually moribund for some time. During the year Cole had approached Lord Derby, who had been President of the Royal Commission of the Great Exhibition, with a view to persuading the Commissioners to help, but to no avail; it was this rebuff that decided Cole to go it alone. He wrote to the Queen's Private Secretary, General Charles Grey, with whom he was acquainted, to enlist his support and influence with the Prince. Grey was only too pleased to assist and at the end of 1864 he notified Cole that he had approached the Queen on the matter and she had expressed a wish that not only should the Prince be President of the Committee but also play an active part in getting the Hall erected; further the Prince himself had agreed to carry out his Mother's wishes. As a result of Grey's successful intervention the Commissioners changed their minds and in 1865 decided to contribute a quarter of the building cost, up to a maximum of £50,000 provided the remaining finance required was raised within eighteen months; this offer meant in effect that the Commissioners found themselves holders of 500 "Perpetual free admission" seats!

From this point in mid-1865 money began to flow in, various sub-committees of the Provisional Committee were established—Advice, which dealt with the Hall's design, Charter, Finance, Organ and Prospectus respectively dealing with the subjects of their titles—and Fowke prepared detailed plans of the interior. However, before he had progressed any further than rough sketches for the exterior, he died of a heart attack in December, 1865. His successor was the Secretary of the Provisional Committee, Scott, an extraordinary choice and one which certainly would never be made in similar circumstances today; for Scott was not a professional architect though an amateur of considerable talent. To entrust him with a scheme of such size, complexity and prestige must have cast some doubt on the wisdom of the Provisional Committee but in the end it turned out to be a justifiable decision. Scott wasted no time after his appointment and in the space of a few months produced fresh plans basing them on Fowke's proposals but amending and altering them to suit his own ideas and those of the Advice Committee which had been formed after Fowke's death with the object of being a sort of watchdog over Scott's activities. This Committee was composed of James Fergusson, John Fowler, John Hawkshaw, Richard Redgrave, R.A., Sir W. Tite, M.P. and Sir M. Digby Wyatt, F.S.A.

By 20th May 1867, the day of the laying of the foundation stone, over £100,200 had been subscribed and this, coupled with the £50,000 promised by the Commissioners, meant that the finances were three quarters of the way towards the target of £200,000. If Scott's appointment as architect was unconventional then the finding of the remaining quarter of the finances required was even more bizarre. The firm of Lucas Bros., which had built the 1862 Exhibition Centre, Liverpool Street Station and the Royal Albert Docks, stated that if its tender was accepted it would guarantee the outstanding financial balance by taking up the amount in the form of seats in the Hall. This offer was accepted and the contract let without going out to open tender, a procedure nowadays likely to raise questions in the House and be the subject of an enquiry into its morality, apart from its possible financial implications. Indeed Scott made a most revealing comment when writing to Grey about a last minute hitch concerning the method of payment to the contractors—"£180,000 would build the Hall complete if we could proceed by open tender." Further he even suggested the possibility of approaching the firm of Smith & Taylor, which was at the time building the Albert Memorial, and in fact did so but when Lucas Bros. realised what was afoot the difficulties soon withered away and the contract drawn up and accepted, though paradoxically it was not formally signed for another two years. The figure agreed upon was £199,748, just £252 less than the maximum permitted to guarantee the Commissioners' grant of £50,000. Such accuracy was not providential and drastic pruning had occurred to get the amount down from the quantity surveyors', Hunt, Stephenson & Jones, original concept of £235,000.

Scott was appointed Director of Works with an honorarium of £6,000 and on 9th April 1867, the day following acceptance of the contract, work commenced on the site.

CHAPTER TWO

Construction and the first thirty years

ON 20th May 1867 the Queen laid the foundation stone. Most of the excavations had been completed and a large marquee was erected over the area to shelter the 6,000 guests. A platform had been erected and on each side was an enclosure, one for government ministers and the other for members of the Diplomatic Corps, the rest of the marquee being occupied with rows of less comfortable seats.

Just before 11.30 a.m. the Prince of Wales and the Duke of Edinburgh took their places on the platform. The Queen travelled by train from Windsor to Paddington where she transferred to an open carriage for the drive through Hyde Park to join the Royal brothers, the Princesses Louise and Beatrice and the Home Secretary, Gathorne Hardy, on the platform. After a short speech of welcome by the Prince of Wales and the presentation by him of a formal address from the Provisional Committee the Queen replied in a voice quiet and full of emotion:-

> ''I thank you for your affectionate and dutiful address'', she said. ''It has been with a struggle that I have nerved myself to a compliance with the wish that I should take part in this day's ceremony; but I have been sustained by the thought that I should assist by my presence in promoting the accomplishment of his great designs to whose memory the gratitude and affection of the country is now rearing a noble monument, which I trust may yet look down on such a centre of institutions for the promotion of art and science as it was his fond hope to establish here. It is my wish that this hall should bear his name to whom it will have owed its existence, and be called 'The Royal Albert Hall of Arts and Sciences'.''

Her Majesty then accepted from the Prime Minister, the Earl of Derby, some gold and silver coins and a dedicatory inscription which she placed in a glass vessel handed to her by the Lord President of the Council, Earl Granville. She then placed the vessel in a cavity over which the inscribed stone of red Aberdeen granite was lowered and which she ceremoniously laid with a golden trowel and ebony and ivory gavel presented to her by Charles Lucas on behalf of the building contractors; this to the accompaniment of a fanfare by trumpeters of the Life Guards and a 21 gun salute by a battery of the Royal Horse Artillery in Hyde Park. The stone is now situated in the stalls behind two seats in the back row of 'K' Block on the right hand side facing the organ and consequently is difficult to see. To conclude the proceedings the Archbishop of Canterbury intoned the Lord's Prayer and gave the benediction. Then followed the Prince Consort's own composition, *L'invocazione all' Armonia*, rendered by Giovanni Mario and the Covent Garden Italian Opera Company conducted by Michael Costa.

Even as building progressed, however, controversy still raged, ranging from amateur architect Scott to the function of the building when it was completed; from points of heating, lighting and ventilation to maintenance and running costs and above all to the design. In spite of it all work went on apace with few problems or interruptions though two early difficulties did arise, both connected with water. The first was when a spring or underground stream was encountered and had to be diverted by means of a conduit, and the second occurred when it was discovered that the external wall would at one point pass over the top of a well which supplied the Horticultural Gardens; this necessitated increasing the thickness of the foundations at the point to 30 feet. The subterranean flow of water is something of a mystery but is believed to be a tributary of the Westbourne Stream. In the basement today there is a manhole giving direct

Queen Victoria laying the foundation stone of the Royal Albert Hall on 20th May 1867. A large marquee had been erected over the site to shelter the 6,000 guests. *Royal Albert Hall*

access many feet below to the water which can clearly be heard flowing when the cover is removed.

On 7th November 1867 Henry Cole's wife laid the first of an estimated six million bricks with an inscribed silver trowel, now displayed, along with the ivory handled ebony gavel used by the Queen to lay the foundation stone, in a glass case in the General Manager's office.

Perhaps the most interesting feature of an impressive exterior, largely buff on a chocolate ground with black outlines, is the mosaic frieze which encircles the building at a height of 100 feet and is some 800 feet in length. It comprises an assembly of allegorical groups which a consortium of artists had been asked to design in 50 feet lengths. It covers an area of about 5,200 square feet and cost £4,426, a remarkably reasonable figure in view of the work involved and the number of people employed; of this sum £3,444 was expended on labour and materials, £782 on artists' fees and £200 on the work of a Sergeant in the Royal Engineers, Spackman by name, who photographed the designs and then made enlargements from which female students working in the South Kensington Museum assembled millions of tiny tesserae into six and a half feet high panels, taking two years over their task. A description of these panels is given in Appendix Four. Above the frieze are the following series of inscriptions:—

THIS HALL WAS ERECTED FOR THE ADVANCEMENT OF
THE ARTS AND SCIENCES AND WORKS OF INDUSTRY OF
ALL NATIONS IN FULFILMENT OF THE INTENTION OF
ALBERT PRINCE CONSORT.

THE SITE WAS PURCHASED WITH THE PROCEEDS OF
THE GREAT EXHIBITION OF THE YEAR MDCCCLI.

THE FIRST STONE OF THE HALL WAS LAID BY HER
MAJESTY QUEEN VICTORIA ON THE TWENTIETH DAY
OF MAY MDCCCLXVII AND IT WAS OPENED BY HER
MAJESTY THE TWENTY-NINTH OF MARCH IN THE
YEAR MDCCCLXXI.

THINE O LORD IS THE GREATNESS AND THE POWER AND
THE GLORY AND THE VICTORY AND THE MAJESTY
FOR ALL THAT IS IN THE HEAVEN AND IN THE EARTH
IS THINE.

THE WISE AND THEIR WORKS ARE IN THE HAND OF
GOD. GLORY BE TO GOD ON HIGH AND ON EARTH PEACE.

One of the trickiest design problems that Scott had faced was that of the double-domed roof which was the largest and loftiest of its type in the world when erected, supported only at the circumference; in this respect he worked in close cooperation with the structural engineers, Ordish & Grover. Manufacture and construction was undertaken at the Manchester works of the Fairbairn Engineering Company which erected the whole contrivance on the ground and subjected it to a thorough testing before dismantling it and sending it to London by road. The roof structure, containing some 400 tons of metal, was firmly in position in May, 1869 and on the eleventh of the month Scott and Grover, after ordering everyone out of the building, removed the wedges which separated the central elliptical ring from the girders which had all previously been bolted together; the ring dropped a mere 5/16 of an inch.

Eighteen months later work had advanced to the extent that it was deemed desirable to invite the Queen to inspect the project as it neared completion. This she did on 3rd December 1870 accompanied by Princess Beatrice but without Grey who had died the previous March, so depriving Cole of the second of the accomplices who had done some much in the face of considerable adversity and disappointment. Fowke and Grey did not live to savour the success they had struggled so hard to achieve and Cole must have had many regrets that they had not survived to share his triumph at the grand opening ceremony. Cole, Scott and Thomas Lucas showed Victoria over the building; she seemed well pleased with her visit and remarked that it "Looks like the British Constitution." For the first time she sat in the Royal Box and even visited the Balcony; from both points she was able to try out the acoustics because Cole had arranged for a Mr. Healy to play the violin and a Miss Williams and a Mr. Britten to sing a few songs to demonstrate the Hall's sound qualities, or lack of them.

Acoustics is a problem which bedevilled the Hall right from the start and has, as will be seen later, only been satisfactorily resolved in recent years. On 25th February 1871 the first full-scale sound test was carried out when some 7,000 people were assembled for a free performance by an amateur musical society, the Wandering Minstrels, conducted by the Hon. Seymour Egerton. The result was disconcerting to say the least, with echoes here, reverberations there, "blind" spots elsewhere and excellent hearing in some parts. To mitigate the worst defects a calico velarium was suspended below the dome and did service for so long that when it was removed on 6th July 1949 over a ton of dust, which took eight large vacuum-cleaners a day and a half to collect, went with it. Scott's opinion on acoustical problems was that "They are like strategy; the principles are soon mastered but the difficulty lies in their application, which difficulty is to be overcome by experience." This military analogy was apposite since Scott was to end his service career with the rank of major-general.

The next Royal visitors welcomed by Cole were the Prince of Wales, Princess Alexandra, the Prince Consort's brother, the Duke of Saxe-Coburg-Gotha, and Prince Arthur. Their visit occurred on 23rd March 1871, only six days before the official opening, and yet work still was being feverishly pursued day and night and was to continue right up to and beyond the opening ceremony.

On 28th March a rehearsal of the concert to be performed the following day was held, attended by Prince Arthur and the Duke of Teck; once again the acoustics were put to the test and found wanting, Costa, now Sir Michael, who conducted the 1,200 performers, expressing disgust at the flatness of the sound.

Opposite: Trial erection of the double-domed roof by the Fairbairn Engineering Company.

Right: The roof in position as construction of the hall goes ahead in 1869.

Royal Albert Hall

During the later stages of construction there had been a serious fire risk as the men worked with the aid of candles secured to benches and tables with their own wax or placed in bottle necks. That night, as scores of men worked through the hours of darkness to get as much done as possible before the following day's ceremony, there was a genuine fire scare which brought crowds flocking to what was thought might well be a conflagration which would not only put paid to the ceremony but to the Hall as well. Fortunately the blaze was in the contractor's workshops adjoining the Hall, the fire coinciding with the testing of the gas lighting installation inside the building. This was something to behold, approximately 11,000 burners, enclosed in gold coloured chandeliers, being ignited in ten seconds by an electric spark in each cluster. To combat the consequences of a possible fire fifteen water tanks each of 1,400 gallons capacity were positioned in the Gallery; they were fed by pumping water from a 430 feet deep artesian well originally constructed to supply the Royal Horticultural Society's conservatory and gardens and in use until October, 1907, since when supplies have been obtained from the Metropolitan Water Board.

The ventilation and heating of such an enormous building also posed many problems for the engineer, Wilson W. Phipson. The difficulties were finally overcome by the construction of a pair of widely spaced shafts with apertures at some distance from the Hall; through these air was conveyed to the building, being strained by fine sieves and passed through water-sprays. It was then driven into the main air-chambers by a couple of fans operating on the screw principle; each had four blades and together were capable of forcing 3½ million cubic feet per hour into the building. The air was warmed in chambers in the basement, being heated to about 150°F (66°C) by steam generated in three 25 h.p. tubular boilers. About 27,000 feet of four inch diameter piping was used in the chambers and by driving the air about inside more or less any temperature could be achieved. The air was conducted by means of flues in the walls to all parts of the building and by an arrangement of valves the external air could be driven in by the fans without passing between the pipes and so it was possible to regulate the temperature to any required level. The action of the fans was supplemented by a powerful exhaust shaft, with an area of 130 sq. ft., in the ceiling and passing through beyond the highest point of the roof. A strong upward current in the shaft was produced by about 1,260 gas-jets which heated the exhausted air, thus causing it to rise and be discharged harmlessly into the atmosphere. This wondrous and intricate system was made to excel itself at the opening ceremony when the air pumped into the Hall was perfumed with Eau-de-Cologne.

On the great day it was fortunate that the heating system was on its best behaviour. The weather was bitterly cold and cloudy with a cutting East wind but the populace turned out in their thousands to line the streets from Buckingham Palace to the Hall to witness the Royal progress in a procession of nine carriages

Queen Victoria arriving for the state opening of the Royal Albert Hall on 29th March 1871.

escorted by the 1st Life Guards and obtain a rare view of the Monarch who was still secluding herself from the public nearly ten years after Albert's death. Once again she was in deep mourning, the only concession to the all pervading black being some white flowers on her bonnet tied with black and white ribbons. There was all the customary panoply that accompanies state occasions; troop-lined streets, escorts, guards-of-honour and bands all resplendent in full-dress uniform, including the Yeoman of the Guard who lined the crimson cloth covered gangway placed in the Arena from beneath the Royal Box to the platform in front of the orchestra; outside the main entrance the guard of honour was mounted by the Queen's colour company of the Coldstream Guards with the regimental band.

That morning official guests and seat holders started to take their places soon after 10 o'clock and they were joined by ordinary members of the public, the more affluent of whom had paid £25. 4s. (£25.20) for an eight seater Box or three guineas (£3.15) for a reservation in the Stalls; others contented themselves with either a two-guinea (£2.10) seat in the Balcony or a guinea (£1.05) seat in the Gallery. Seatholders paid only 50% of these rates. The whole assembly presented a colourful setting to match the importance of the occasion. The familiar scene today of an orchestra and chorus forming up on the platform below the organ was enacted in public for the first time when 500 players were joined by 1,200 members of the Sacred Harmonic Society supplemented by groups from the Handel Festival and Crystal Palace Choirs. For some reason apparently never made clear the Band of the Grenadier Guards conducted by Dan Godfrey entertained the gathering from behind red curtains filling three of the Gallery archways at the rear of the organ. Just about everybody that was anybody in the life of the capital were present, including the Duke of Cambridge, in the Field-Marshal's uniform of Commander-in-Chief, and the

The opening of the Royal Albert Hall on 29th March, 1871. *Illustrated London News*

Prince and Princess of Teck in the Prince of Wales' Box; the Prime Minister, William Ewart Gladstone and members of his Government; Benjamin Disraeli and other members of the Opposition; a fine array of the Services, aristocracy and Diplomatic Corps and many representatives of business, the professions and learned societies, and mayors of over 50 towns which had contributed at least a hundred guineas (£105) to the Great Exhibition.

By now the assembly was almost complete and Cole came onto the platform to request stillness so that a photographer of the London Stereoscopic Company could record the scene for posterity. At 12.30 the Queen was received at the main entrance by the Prince of Wales in the uniform of the 10th Hussars and the procession then formed in readiness for entry to the Arena and the walk to the platform. This had been placed in the centre of the Auditorium, was covered with a dark red carpet and surmounted by a gold fringed and tasselled purple velvet canopy which had last seen similar duty when Victoria and Albert were present at the opening of the Great Exhibition nearly 20 years previously. Leading the procession were the Lord President of the Council, Earl Granville, and the Home Secretary, Henry Austin Bruce, followed by Henry Cole and the Lucas brothers, representatives of the Commissioners and Provisional Committee, the Duke of Saxe-Coburg-Gotha in Austrian officer's uniform, Princess Alexandra, Prince Arthur in the uniform of the Rifle Brigade and the Princesses Louise and Beatrice. Then came Prince Leopold in Highland dress, Prince Christian in General's uniform, Princess Christian and the Marquis of Lorne in the uniform of a captain in the Highlanders and who had married Princess Louise only eight days earlier at Windsor. Finally came the Queen and as she entered the Auditorium the assembly rose and cheered and Dr William Thomas Best at the organ and the Grenadier Guards Band played the National Anthem. The Queen then proceeded to the platform where she joined the other members of the Royal family and her entourage and seated herself on a gilt and crimson damask throne. The Prince of Wales then read an address of welcome before handing the document to Her Majesty who replied with a brevity that did not really fit the occasion. After receiving the formal reply from the Home Secretary she passed it to the Prince, merely saying "In handing you this answer, I have to express my great admiration for this beautiful Hall, and my earnest wishes for its complete success." The Queen's remarkably brief peroration was followed by more cheering and the saying of a prayer by the Bishop of London, Dean of the Chapels Royal, officiating in place of the Archbishop of Canterbury who was ill. Now the moment had arrived for Her Majesty to declare the Hall open she was so overcome by the proceedings that she was unable to do so. There was a hurried whispered conversation between her and the Prince before he announced simply—"The Queen declares this Hall now open." The brevity of Victoria's vocal contribution to the events did not allay any of the enthusiasm and once more the crowd got to its feet and cheered and again the National

Anthem was played, this time by the organ, orchestra and trumpeters conducted by Costa. One trumpeter had been stationed outside the Hall so that he could be a link between the Anthem being played in the Hall and the officer in command of a battery of the Royal Horse Artillery at Knightsbridge Barracks which fired a 21-gun salute as the ceremony drew to a close. The addresses of the Prince of Wales and Her Majesty and the Bishop of London's prayer are given in Appendix Two.

An interior view of the opening ceremony. *Illustrated London News*

The Queen and her party then retired to the Royal Box to listen to a cantata, described as *Handelian in texture*, specially composed for the occasion by Costa, who had set the music to words arranged by John Oxenford from the songs of praise in the Psalms of David.

After the excitement and splendour of the opening ceremony, work was resumed and certainly much remained to be done. The organ, with its nine miles or so of pipes, had been put through its paces to some effect but appeared to be surrounded by a phalanx of scaffolding as a number of poles supported the larger pipes, and the whole instrument and its casing were unpainted. Indeed, decoratively the only parts completed were the ceiling and the arcading immediately below it; the panelling in front of the Boxes had not even been commenced and the bare walls were hung with draperies to hide their deficiencies from the critical eyes of the august assembly.

Perhaps the most surprising thing to become apparent towards the end was the decorative and furnishing hotch potch of the Boxes which had all the beauty and luxury of a series of drawing rooms; individuality and not a little bad taste had run riot. The owners were at liberty to do their own thing in order to satisfy their eccentricities of taste, except for the green carpeting and the crimson outer curtaining which harmonised well with the buff and French grey of the woodwork and the brass fittings and were of course part of the Hall's general embellishment. The owners obviously vied with one another to make ostentation their hallmark regardless of expense; even the Royal Box did not escape this sort of attention but at least the *Morning Post* considered it "artistically pleasing to the vision" with its turquoise blue decorations, gold patra and crimson fringe.

These personalised Boxes have long since disappeared and all now conform to the general overall scheme of red, all that is except Box 38 of the Second Tier which has been retained in its original style. The present owner should be well pleased and satisfied that the Box is the last tenuous link with the idiosyncrasies of a bygone age; it is lavishly ornamented with plaster ovals and relief figures, ribbons and chains, and two walls are panelled with mirrors. Even the Royal Box, which is in effect Boxes 27 and 28 of the Grand Tier, conforms to the general decorative and furnishing trend unless actually being used by the Royal Family when, as will be seen later, there is a transformation. Decoratively speaking the only original portion left is tucked away in one of the store rooms—a small area of one wall having a design in red on a greyish-green background.

As might have been expected the completed building came in for plenty of criticism; Italian Renaissance style is not everyone's ideal of structural and decorative elegance and it was likened to a huge bandbox, a gasometer, a St. Pancras engine shed and a wedding cake from which the top tier had been blown across Kensington Gore onto the Albert Memorial. It has been described further as only fit for bull fights or gladiatorial combat but, considerably more complimentary, the arrangement of the interior has been compared to the works of Paolo Veronese, the great 16th century Italian artist, one of whose specialities was the painting of magnificent buildings. Externally it has been likened to a cross between the Colosseum in Rome and the Rotunda at Ranelagh, which may or may not be complimentary depending on an individual's personal architectural viewpoint. Again comparison has been made to La Scala, Milan, the allusion being that the Hall is more like an opera house than a concert hall; it was called the Kensington Music Hall by Sir Robert Peel, a little more flattering than the Kensington Mausoleum or more succinctly, just "a monstrosity," but nothing like the refinement of "the finest building in Europe since the Pantheon." From the viewpoint of the author of this book the Hall's likeness to a Yorkshire Pie is quite the most intriguing since, though born and bred in that great county, he has never had the good fortune to come across this delicacy.

In spite of all the derisory innuendo the fact remains that it is a magnificent structure just as appropriate to the London scene of the second Elizabethan age as it was symbolic of the Victorian era. The elliptical shape has an extreme short diameter of 238 feet and a long diameter of 272 feet; the height to the roof springing is 135 feet and that to the top of the lantern 150 feet. The minimum roof span is 185 feet 4 inches and the maximum 219 feet 4 inches whilst the ellipse is 332 feet and the distance between porches 338 feet. All these are considerable measurements but still leave the Hall only about one quarter the size of the Colosseum. From basement to roof there are a pair of concentric circuits of walls 20 feet apart, whilst for half the height of the building there is a third concentric wall nine feet from the inner main wall, which supports the enormous roof structure of nearly half an acre of glass fixed in the iron framework.

The red Fareham brick walls have decorations and facings of buff Tamworth terra-cotta which also forms a 13 feet high base right round the perimeter in which are shield-shaped panels of monograms and heraldic emblems; the window surrounds and keystones are decorated with crowns and the Royal monogram. The four rectangular porches to the main entrances project beyond the face of the elliptical wall and have arches which originally enabled passengers to alight from their carriages under cover. The North entrance faces onto Kensington Gardens and the Albert Memorial and has a pair of niches which were intended to hold statues of Victoria and Albert though in fact they have never done; above the portico is a room once used as a lecture theatre but nowadays accommodating the Central Refreshment Bar. Originally the South entrance was connected to the conservatory of the Horticultural Society's Gardens, access being gained by two flights of steps, but this arrangement has long since disappeared; it also differs from the other entrances in that there is not a room above. The East and West porticos lack a central arch, the walls being built up and relieved by three window openings filled with ornamental iron grilles; over the East portico is a room once used for lectures, then a printing shop and now just as storage accommodation; the room over the West portico was originally a theatre with a seating capacity of 252, a stage with a height of 14 feet 6 inches, a width of 40 feet 2 inches, a depth of 18 feet 4 inches and a 21 feet 10 inches wide proscenium arch. Seven of the ten rows of seats actually occupied the 20 feet wide space between the two outer concentric walls of the main building but this incursion stopped in 1958 when the theatre ceased to be used for performances after some 80 years of service. It is now the Balcony Restuarant.

A prominent feature of the upper part of the building is an outer balcony with ornamental balustrade some 90 feet above ground level, running entirely round the perimeter and so complementing the Gallery inside from which it is accessible.

As the great edifice moved into tentative stride as a cultural and social outlet for the capital's growing population, the Council was not slow to foster the initial interest which had followed the long years of the Hall's building, culminating in the splendid Royal occasion of its opening. The doors were thrown open for public inspection of the magnificence within when performances were not in progress, sixpence (2½p) per head being charged for the privilege, a sum which did not deter 44,000 people from accepting the offer the following year.

The Council had succeeded the Provisional Committee which voted itself out of existence twelve months after the opening ceremony in accordance with the terms of the Charter. During that period, however, the Committee had to address itself to getting the Hall into a profit-making groove and onto a sound business footing. The insurance cover certainly did not show much business acumen by the Committee since only half of the building cost was deemed adequate—an apparently extraordinary state of affairs when the high fire risk alone is considered. Fire, in fact, was a continuing source of concern to many

The Royal Albert Hall when first built, seen from the Horticultural Gardens.
Illustrated London News

people for a number of years though the Council merely carried on where the Committee left off and was just as complacent.

If the Committee was not fully aware of its insurance obligations it did at least do much better in other financial directions, starting with an agreement whereby the Commissioners paid £3,000 annually in return for being able to mount artistic and scientific exhibitions in the Gallery; as the arrangement was for a term of three years it was a useful launching pad for the money raising process, especially as the usage was to be only for a five month period each year, from the beginning of May to the end of September.

From 1878 Fine Arts Exhibitions were held in the Gallery where the lighting was particularly suitable for the display of oil and water colour paintings, enamelware, pottery, terra-cotta works, bronzes, wood carvings, engravings and lithography. Up to 24,000 visitors a week were recorded and the Queen even put in an appearance.

Exhibitions of one sort or another became in fact quite commonplace and throughout the 1880s the Gallery, with its abundant ambulatory space, shared these enterprises with the Horticultural Society's Gardens. There was a Fisheries Exhibition, International Health and Inventions Exhibitions, an Anglo-Danish Exhibition and Ecclesiastical Art and Works of Art applied to Furniture Exhibitions. The International Cookery Exhibition had the grandiose title of "Salon Culenaire" and ranged, as the advertisements proclaimed, "from fois gras to plain." There was also a display of pictures temporarily displaced from the Grosvenor Gallery. The Colonial and Indian Exhibition of 1886 was opened by the Queen, in honour of which Lord Tennyson wrote an ode which was set to music by Sir Arthur Sullivan and sung by Emma Albani and a choir. One of the attractions of the Inventions Exhibition was the twice weekly demonstration of the Maxim automatic machine gun firing fully-loaded service cartridges!

Within a year of the first of these exhibitions electric lighting was installed on a limited scale and on 13 February 1879 it was used for the first time at a concert but nine more years were to elapse before the Theatre, Boxes and Auditorium were illuminated by the new system, installed by the Anglo-American British Electric Light Corporation. Perhaps it was more than coincidence that the initial lighting installation came at the same time as the first ever organised display of electric lighting equipment. The principal exhibits were on show in the Arena with the Gallery being used for the demonstration of specialist equipment for dentistry and surgery. The opening ceremony was performed by the Prince of Wales who, after attending a lecture on electricity, toured the exhibition and then listened to an organ recital.

1896 was another year when a new invention came to the Hall though it did not stand the test of time. The Electrophone Company, for a fee of £50 per annum, was prepared to install on a subscriber's premises an apparatus which had a dialling system similar to that of a modern telephone and enabled a person to listen to events in certain of the capital's halls and theatres and the Royal Albert Hall became one of the favoured establishments. What reception was like is not known and neither is there a record whether subscribers were favoured with the famous echo, though the same year, Wentworth Lindsay Cole, who had been appointed the Hall's first general manager 20 years previously and was a nephew of Henry Cole, had an idea which apparently helped considerably to reduce the echo nuisance. He had wires stretched across the Hall and suspended rabbit netting from each—primitive and unsightly maybe but quite effective, so we are told.

Henry himself did not live to see the full impact of the electric lighting nor his nephew's efforts at acoustical improvement. He died in April, 1882, something of an eccentric in his old age but nevertheless with the honour of a knighthood, bestowed on 26th March 1875; he received the accolade at Windsor Castle on 7th December of the same year.

The musical side of affairs had always been uppermost in Henry Cole's mind and now was the time to start to put his desires into tangible form. From the beginning a tradition was founded that has grown and prospered right down to the present day

About four and a half thousand people attended the first concert on 12th April 1871 and no doubt luxuriated in the new fangled revolving seats in the Amphitheatre or the tip-up seats in the Balcony. It was organised as one of a series of six by the Society of Arts to raise money for the founding of a National Training School for Music, which eventually became the Royal College of Music. Mainly popular works were played during the series, including three overtures per concert, and drew a lot of adverse notices from the critics. A miscellany of organisations hired the Hall to stage their own performances, the most prominent being the Sacred Harmonic Society which put on four oratorios in the first two months. One of the earliest hopes of Cole and his confederates was not only that the Hall should be a vast affair capable of accommodating audiences of many thousands, but also that it should be a mecca for performances given by mass orchestral and choral forces supplemented by the prodigious capabilities of the organ. The ideal was to have a resident choir—a Royal Albert Hall Choir—and this ideal now came to fruition as a result of a minor repercussion of the Franco-Prussian War of 1870/71. Charles François Gounod came to England as a refugee and, though he only stayed five years, did much to put the Hall on the musical map. Composer of several oratorios and the well-known operas *Faust* and *Romeo and Juliet* and the more trifling but popular *Ave-Maria* and *Funeral March of a Marionette*, he had the advantage of having been for some time one of Victoria's favourite composers and this may have had something to do with his being asked to form a large choir out of the National Choral Society which had been founded in 1860 but was numerically incapable of doing justice to itself when performing in the Hall.

Gounod soon set to work and in a very short time got the number up to over a thousand and though several performances were given in 1871 the Choir's biggest moment was when it appeared at the concert inaugurating the International Exhibition which was opened on 1st May by the Prince of Wales in the Royal Horticultural Society's premises next door. By the time it closed five months later there had been flower, fruit and vegetable shows, an international drawing and painting competition, a military band competition, organ recitals, oratorio performances and orchestral and choral concerts in which the Choir was heavily and capably involved. Certainly the Commissioners must have been well pleased with what they had seen and heard because later in the year when the Deputy Music Commissioner, Earl Wilton, proposed the formation of a permanent Royal Albert Hall Choir they made a grant of £5,000 and issued a prospectus asking for volunteers. Membership soon rose to 1,400 and by October, the Royal Albert Hall Choral Society was in business. The participants were of course all amateurs but they were treated well by the Commissioners and were recipients of a number of not unconsidered trifles in lieu of wages or salary.

Also during that first year an international flavour was added to the music making when three concerts were given by the Band of the Belgian Royal Regiment of Guides in late Spring. Then in August there was a Grand Opera Concert and Afternoon Promenade in the Gardens and Hall and in the Autumn several concerts were given by the London Glee and Madrigal Union. Even so promoters were reluctant to hire the Hall when 1,341 of the best seats were denied them, a reluctance that lasted a long time. That the figure was as low as that was entirely due to the Commissioners purchasing the 300 seats owned by Lucas Bros., for £30,000, so increasing their holding of seats to 800, and then agreeing that these could be let by the Corporation or its lessees subject only that two-sevenths of the net profits, if any, should accrue to the Commissioners. In addition a further 250 seats were offered for sale but only 141 sold.

25th March 1872 was the date on which the Provisional Committee ceased to exist and the newly constituted Council took over the reins of looking after and further promoting the well-being of the Hall. The eighteen-man Council, which met for the first time on 13th April, was the governing body of the equally newly constituted Corporation of which every seat-holder was a member, having one vote for each seat held. The Prince of Wales was President of the Corporation and as such an ex-officio member of the Council. He was also given powers of appointing four Vice Presidents annually. The Council started by possessing some continuity with the Provisional Committee since six members of the latter were immediately elected to the former. The constitution provided that six members should resign annually but could be available for re-election. As a result a sort of "closed shop" prevailed; in practice those that had to retire each year were usually re-elected, resulting in a situation that the Council was sadly lacking in new blood from year to year unless death removed a member.

The Council's first meeting was under the chairmanship of the Senior Vice President, the Duke of Edinburgh; the other members were Earl Granville, K.G.; Earl Faversham, Rt. Hon. Lord Clarence Edward Paget, K.C.B.; Major-General Sir Thomas Myddleton Biddulph, M.P.; Thomas Baring, M.P.; Edgar Alfred Bowring, C.B., M.P.; Edward Lyall Brandreth; Henry Cole, C.B.; Warren Delarue, F.R.S.; Captain John Frecheville Dykes Donnelly, R.E. (Secretary); John Fowler; Charles James Freake; John Hawkshaw, F.R.S., (Treasurer); Henry Arthur Hunt, C.B.; Dr Lyon Playfair, C.B., M.P.; Henry Cadogan Rothery; and Major-General Henry Young Darracott Scott, C.B.

The new mood was set straight away by the Duke's comment:- "The principal objects of this meeting are to place the Hall on a sound basis—one of self support, with a prospect of just sufficient gain to ensure maintenance and gradual improvements." To achieve these necessary and worthwhile targets rental charges were set three months later at £30 for each daytime and £50 for each evening engagement, £5 extra being charged for each quarter of an hour after 11 p.m. In addition to these basic rates 15% of the gross receipts was charged and the Council reserved the right of sale of all tickets. For concerts given by the Royal Albert Hall Choral Society the 15% charge on gross receipts was increased to 25%. Eighteen concerts by the Society were decided upon in addition to 40 orchestral concerts which were to include a number for the working classes at a charge of one penny (0.416p). The Duke was a talented musician himself so it can fairly be said that so far as that particular form of art was concerned he led from the front. Later in the year the Council agreed to form an orchestra of amateur musicians which flourished under the title of the Royal Albert Hall Amateur Orchestral Society, with the Duke as its President. It was a direct complement to the Royal Albert Hall Choral Society and gave its first concert in 1873, one of the concerts being attended by the Princess Alexandra and other members of the Royal Family. The concerts were mostly in aid of charities such as for those bereaved by the Ashanti War and for the establishment of Baths and Wash Houses for the poor of the East End. For a time its President played among the first violins and it is on record that he once played Handel's *Largo* accompanied only by his personal harpist, John Cheshire, who was the last person to hold this Royal appointment.

On 8th May 1872, only six weeks after the Corporation took control, the Choral Society presented its first concert and the occasion was honoured by the presence of the Queen, the Princesses Beatrice and Christian and the German Empress. It might be thought that such an auspicious and distinguished event would have been all sweetness and light but the programme came in for a lot of criticism on the grounds that all the items except the *Hallelujah Chorus* from Handel's *Messiah* had been "arranged" by the conductor, Gounod. The following three concerts brought forth the same sort of condemnation and eventually led to Gounod's resignation after the Council refused to let him

promote a concert of his own because he proposed including popular items to draw a vast audience, having deliberately refrained from including similar selections when the concerts were put on by the Council. The financial effect of all the fuss was disastrous, a deficit of £3,000 being accumulated at the end of the year. With Gounod's departure the Council had to find another conductor and Joseph Barnby was selected. This factor and the decision to appoint a firm of professional managers, Novello, Ewer and Company, to be responsible for the concerts turned the tide. The first performance under the new regime took place on 12th February 1873, was successful and led to further encouraging results later in the season.

As concert succeeded concert some made a profit and some made a loss but generally speaking they were attracting larger and larger audiences and the public was slowly encouraged and persuaded that the trek out to South Kensington was really worth the effort and the Royal Albert Hall was the place to go for musical performances of quality. Popular works were not always the attraction either since during the 1870s Bach, Handel, Haydn and Mendelssohn oratorios—the *Christmas Oratorio*, the *St. Matthew Passion*, *Messiah*, *Samson*, *Judas Maccabaeus*, *Israel in Egypt*, *Belshazzar*, *Theodora*, the *Creation* and *Elijah*—were regularly presented. The *St. Matthew Passion* was given on successive nights in Holy Week and audiences were invited to stand and join in the singing of the choral or metrical hymns; to give the necessary cues a trumpeter would appear at the appropriate times at the head of each of the dozen staircases to the Auditorium.

However, just as man cannot live by bread alone it was soon realised that

Opposite: The inscribed silver trowel with which Lady Cole laid the first brick and the ivory handled ebony gavel used by the Queen to lay the foundation stone.

Right: The foundation stone laid by Queen Victoria, now hidden by the seats in the back row of 'K' block.
Royal Albert Hall

the Hall could not exist by music alone. One of the difficulties facing the Council in its search for financial stability was the necessity of keeping within the terms of the Hall's Charter and this posed certain problems as to what could or could not be presented. Within four months of the Hall's opening, the City Middle Class School held its Speech-Day celebrations in the Hall and a year later the Society of Telegraph Engineers and Commissioners successfully demonstrated to the amazement of onlookers an ink-writing morse apparatus. Messages were exchanged between the Hall and Karachi via Persia (Iran) which gave an opportunity to the Grand Vizier of that country to send a message to the Prince of Wales. These events could of course be easily gathered under the arts and sciences umbrella but what of a consignment of Portugese wine to be displayed at the 1874 Exhibition? The wine was placed in the Hall's cellars and completely overlooked until too late. The producers naturally were aggrieved and had to be placated so it was decided the wine should be used up at a series of luncheons; these resulted in the formation of a wine club which quickly developed into the International Exhibition Co-operative Wine Society Ltd. Cole ingeniously got round the small difficulty of the Hall's Charter by the justification that "Wines involve chemistry, natural history and the art of using the grape. The cellars may thus, I think, be said to have been used for Science and Art."

This tongue-in-cheek interpretive stretching of the Charter was to achieve a new and preposterous height in 1875 and was particularly reprehensible in more ways than one. On 24th January the Grand Secretary of the United Order of English Freemasons, John Hervey, applied for the use of the Hall on 28th April for the purpose of the installation of the Prince of Wales as Grand Master of the Order. It is highly unlikely that Hervey was unaware of the fact that seat-holders had the right to attend any or all of the events held in the Hall and even if he was the Prince, as President of the Council, certainly would be cognisant of the fact. Hervey, with amazing effrontery and complete lack of regard for the seat-holders' rights, demanded that all the ritual surrounding the activities of the Order should be observed, including strict privacy with admission limited to qualified members, and that only those of the Hall's staff who were members should be permitted to render service. Equally extraordinary was the reaction of one of the Council's Vice Presidents, Lyon Playfair, who did not reply direct to Hervey but instead approached the Prince of Wales, pointing out the difficulties if the seat-holders upheld their undoubted right to attend but that "if the Prince expressed a wish, the Council would be prepared to meet his wishes." The Prince did express a wish and the Hall was let on Hervey's terms. Letters were sent to the seat-holders explaining the position but the hoped-for response was not forthcoming in some instances and there were objections; the Council's response to these was that the complainants were asked to reconsider their attitude in view of "the very exceptional circumstances." Threats were made to obtain an injuction against the Council letting the Hall on the proposed terms but the Council pricked this particular balloon by insisting that the affair was of a private nature, whereas seat-holders could only insist on being present on public occasions. This explanation did the trick and no more was heard of injunctions; the installation went ahead and it was only in the annual report that the Council admitted that seat-holders had all the time the right to attend but it felt justified in the action it had taken in view of it being well known that Masons "allow none but members of their own body to be present at their meetings." Such a deplorable and spineless violation of the Charter might well have involved the Council in litigation either before or after the event but the whole issue was soon forgotten. When the Prince presided at the Jubilee celebrations in 1887 the proceedings passed off without causing the slightest trouble.

The Prince's visit to the Hall in 1876 was much less controversial when he attended a concert in thanksgiving for his safe return from India where he had been on a state visit. He was received by the Council led by his brother, the Duke of Edinburgh, and a Guard of Honour of 120 sailors from the ships of the Royal Navy which had accompanied him on the tour. By now Royal attendances at the Hall were becoming quite frequent and did much to boost the flagging income. These auspicious occasions were triggered off by the concert given at the opening ceremony, which showed a profit of £539. 4s. 7d. (£539.23). On 23rd June 1873 the Shah of Persia (Iran), who was on a state visit, listened to a concert which produced a profit of £1,822 and a similar occasion when Alexander II, Emperor of Russia, was guest of honour, went even better with a profit of

£2,754. 13s. 1d. (£2,754. 65). On 19th March 1874 the Duchess of Edinburgh graced the Hall with her presence and a profit resulted of £1,755. 2s. 9d. (£1,755. 14).

Just over sixteen years after his first visit the Shah, on 5th July 1889, went to the Hall for a concert and during the performance he was seated on a dais in the centre of the Arena surrounded by banks of flowers subtly illuminated by electric lamps concealed within the foliage.

Another splendid occasion was the last Command Performance of Victoria's reign. This was on 9th July 1891 in honour of the state visit of the German Emperor and his Consort. The Emperor's visit was the occasion when advertisements first appeared in an official programme; the idea came from Wentworth Lindsay Cole, Henry Cole's nephew who became General Manager in 1876, although he did not proceed with it until after discussion with the Council's President, the Duke of Edinburgh. Having achieved the Royal blessing he was able to report later that the Hall's finances had prospered to the extent of £100.

Part of the frieze depicting "Astronomy and Navigation," this part having been designed by H. S. Marks, A.R.A.

In spite of the early splendid occasion profits the general financial trend was not a happy one and by the Summer of 1874 there was an accrued loss of £5,735. Ordinary concerts frequently made losses and when a profit was made it was of a derisory amount. The professional management had done little better than the ad hoc amateurs and things were looking desperate when in the Spring of 1874 Novello, Ewer & Co., came up with another proposal over which the Council prevaricated for a few months before acquiescing. It was agreed that Novello's should form a permanent orchestra and run concerts for a minimum of three years, the operating costs and profits, if any, being shared equally between the Council and Novello's.

To say the least the scheme was ambitious, involving a concert each weekday night. The first was given on 7th November 1874 and by the New Year financial failure reduced them to two a week. Sixty two of them were presented and on average each showed a loss of £100 so the scheme was reluctantly abandoned; but not before there had been the first London performance of Verdi's *Requiem* conducted by the composer. In all four performances were given during May, 1875, the first being on the 15th of the month, though there had been a rehearsal three days before in front of an invited audience; not only were the performances a musical success but a financial one as well.

Matters were now getting to a desperate state and it was estimated that to get the Hall out of its difficulties would require an annual profit of at least £5,000 (£2,000 to be set aside for repairs and the balance for maintenance). Figures were easy enough to set down on paper but quite another matter to turn into hard cash. Theatrical performances helped and to this end the Royal Albert Hall Amateur Dramatic Club was formed in 1888 and a French play was produced in the Theatre on 19th April of that year. Though the Theatre was well adapted for private theatricals, matinées musicales and such like, any potential hirer must have been somewhat inhibited by a Council ruling that from the beginning of 1877 the Theatre could not be used at night for theatricals. The cost of renting the Theatre varied in those early days between ten and twenty guineas (£10.50 and £21) depending on the purpose for which it was required; a stock of scenery was available to a hirer if required and was included in the price but anything additional was charged as an extra. Also included was attendance and lighting though these elements were excluded for meetings which cost only two to three guineas (£2.10 to £3.15) for artistic or scientific societies. Meanwhile the Lecture Room or Theatre over the East entrance was being used for lectures, bazaars and meetings, and reading rooms were provided in the Balcony but even with all these efforts to improve the financial position the tide did not turn.

Obviously something more drastic and far reaching was desirable; something that would go far to eradicate the element of chance inherent in promoting an event and then being subject to the whims and fancies of the public for support. So why not fall back on the generosity and sentiment of the dedicated few, those who by their actions had shown an interest, even affection, for the Hall's wellbeing and prosperity? With this in mind it was decided in March, 1874, to approach each seat-holder and put the financial situation

A section of the frieze designed by W. F. Yeames, A.R.A., depicting "Workers in Wood and Brick".

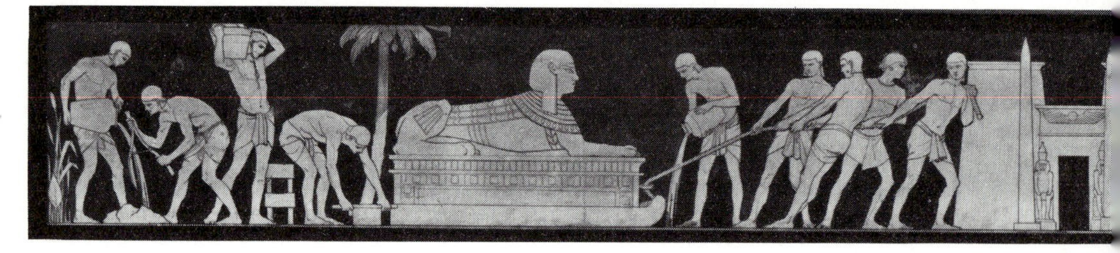

squarely to them. After setting out the stark facts of the case each holder was asked to contribute £3 in respect of each seat held. Any response would of course be of a voluntary nature since there was no legal machinery to make the request mandatory; consequently the appeal was only partially successful. This not being good enough it was agreed in the Summer of the following year that a Bill should be brought before Parliament which if enacted would require all seat-holders to pay £2 per seat per annum and permit the Corporation to purchase any dissenters' seats at their market value.

This proposal, although properly agreed by the majority present at the Annual General Meeting, roused no less a person than Henry Cole to furious indignation. He had strong minority support and a meeting was convened at which a resolution was passed condemning the incompetence of the management in both the past and present and asking for the whole business to be reviewed. Such was the outcry that some not inconsiderable concessions to the original scheme were obtained; these were that the seat rate levy should be a maximum of £2 to be applied for annually by the Council and only be enforceable if passed by a two thirds majority; that there should be no compulsory purchase of seats and the Commissioners' voting rights in respect of the 800 seats they held should be restricted to one vote per 50 seats. Although compulsory purchase was not permitted the Council was empowered to recover any amount due in respect of "the seat rate" by due process for debt through the courts or to let the debtor's seat to a third party, if that were possible, until the debt was redeemed. The Royal Albert Hall Act 1876 received the Royal Assent on 27th June.

The turn of the century was to bring more problems for the Council but it also brought with it more than a touch of sadness. In July, 1900, the Duke of Edinburgh died, followed in October by Wentworth Lindsay Cole and in January, 1901 by Queen Victoria; three individuals so much connected with the successful launching of the Royal Albert Hall had passed away in the space of six months.

"Agriculture", another part of the frieze designed by H. S. Marks, A.R.A.

CHAPTER THREE

Twentieth Century Developments

THE HALL passed into the new century and the Edwardian era with the appointment of Hilton Carter as the new manager, an appointment made only five days after the Queen's death.

Carter was destined to see the Hall change from being a Victorian establishment in the strict sense of the word into something similar to the organisation that is known today, a process hastened by the truncating of a long complex connection between the Hall and the Commissioners of the Exhibition of 1851. Moreover traditions regarding the Hall were clarified out of the realms of uncertainty. The Commissioners were involved with the question of who would pay what proportion for the recently approved South Entrance, and the future of the 800 seats which they still owned. The latter problem was not solved until 1908, when the Commissioners assigned all their seats to the Corporation for the remainder of the long term lease. Although the Corporation lost its annual income it was compensated by having its current debt to the Commissioners wiped out. Perhaps surprisingly the Commissioners agreed to pay the extra amount for the Southern approach and entrance, sixty per cent being viewed as a loan to the Corporation to be repaid in five annual instalments and in 1908 the Commissioners became merely landlords.

It was also in the early years of the century that the removable floor issue reached fruition after years of frustrating debate and procrastination. In 1880 John T. Peacock, one of the trustees appointed under the terms of the 1876 Act, suggested that a removable floor might be erected over the Arena and Amphitheatre Stalls thereby considerably increasing the area available for such things as banquets, bazaars and dances. The idea was not well received at the time but was revived only two years later when plans were prepared and an estimate of £2,000 obtained by a syndicate which was prepared to put up the money. Clearly this gift would add greatly to the Hall's versatility and without any financial obligation devolving on the Corporation. Yet again nothing was done for a further two years when a group of seat-holders resurrected the idea and got as far as obtaining the appointment of a sub-committee to consider the proposal. Urgency certainly did not enter the deliberations and three more years passed before in 1886 three schemes were put forward for discussion.

The great difficulty about these or any other proposals for that matter was that seat-holders' rights would be infringed to the extent that the Stalls would be covered over so making the seating unavailable. As soon as the sub-committee's proposals became known there were objections, even though it was clearly apparent that the Hall's income could be increased considerably if a floor was there for the hiring. Counsel's opinion was sought and unequivocally given—"If any seat-holder's seat is affected, his rights are affected, and it would not be enough to say that the actual seat is untouched if the occupant's use and enjoyment of it were prejudiced . . . For instance, it would be an invasion of the seat-holder's rights to leave his seat at its present level and to raise all his neighbours' seats." This effectively quashed the whole idea since each of the schemes proposed by the sub-committee made provision for the seats that would have been covered to be moved to other parts of the Hall.

The idea of a floor was apparently shelved for ever once Counsel's opinion had been declared and in fact no more was heard of it until 1895 when the Hon. Algernon Bourke had the temerity to suggest that a series of fancy dress balls should be held on a floor specially laid for the purpose but his proposal was rejected on the same grounds that prevailed in the previous decade. The real break-through had to wait another four years when in 1899 a member of the Council, the Earl of Kilmorey, took it upon himself to write to every Corporation member holding seats in the Stalls requesting them to forego their rights for a fortnight in June so that a bazaar could be held in aid of Charing Cross Hospital; each member in return would be entitled to free admission to the bazaar and also to the Sunday concerts which would be held as usual. Whether the charitable appeal of the proposed event coupled with free entry to the bazaar and concerts was the deciding factor will never be known but whatever factor prevailed the result was that the seat-holders did forego their rights and it is pleasing to record that the bazaar was a resounding success.

In spite of the door having been pushed open it is surprising that five years were to elapse before the floor was used again, this time at the instigation of no less a person than the Council President, the Earl of Pembroke and Montgomery. At the end of 1903 he used the same ploy as the Earl of Kilmorey had done in suggesting a charity bazaar, coupled this time with a ball, in aid of another worthy cause, the Victoria Hospital for Children. June again was the selected month and to ease the burden of having to give up their rights temporarily the dispossessed seat-holders were reminded that the first of the two proposed weeks coincided with the racing at Ascot and therefore the Hall would be less of an attraction than it might otherwise have been. Once again charity prevailed and the President's proposal was accepted and as it turned out was decisive. Major-General C. E. Webber, who was a Council member, proposed that the 16,800 square feet of flooring and all its supporting timbers should be purchased by the Corporation and his suggestion was approved with little demur. So it was that the Victoria Hospital's bazaar and ball was the first event to make use of the floor under its new ownership. All the bits and pieces had been numbered by the contractors to facilitate erection, which took 12 carpenters three days to accomplish; the completed structure was 15 feet above the Arena, covered the Stalls seating and butted against the bases of the Loggia Boxes. After the Sunday concert the seats were removed and interlocking parquet blocks laid on the floor and covered with an asbestos carpet on which were erected 26 stalls for the bazaar which lasted three days. The really hectic part of the proceedings then commenced because only three hours was available between the closure of the bazaar and the commencement of the ball; in this short time six of the stalls were dismantled, the asbestos carpet removed and the parquet blocks polished for dancing. The ball finished in the early hours of the morning and then it was necessary to dismantle the remaining 20 stalls, recover the parquet blocks, erect a platform for 500 chairs and place 4,000 more on the floor in readiness for a Salvation Army meeting in the evening. All this was a severe organisational test and apparently was carried out with great expertise; such experience was invaluable for the future when frequently the floor has to be erected and dismantled against the clock.

So far so good but what of the future events that would need the use of the newly acquired floor? The two occasions on which the floor had been utilised were for charitable causes and such considerations were almost certainly the deciding factor for the seat-holders giving their consent; would they be prepared to do likewise when the cause at stake was merely of a business nature? In fact the knowledge of the Hall's parlous financial plight was at last getting through even to the more obdurate and traditional seat-holders who began to realise that unless some substantial improvement was forthcoming in the foreseeable future there might not be a Hall for them to attend. The Supplemental Charter excluded them from their seats on ten occasions each year and now it was put to them that if they agreed to forego the use of their seats for additional lettings they would be offered a share of the profits made from them, though no mention seems to have been made of how possible losses were to be apportioned. In theory such an offer might have been expected to mollify and even satisfy seat-holders deprived of their heritage, but practically if only one of them refused to cooperate then that particular proposed letting would be in jeopardy. Such a situation did indeed happen when the Misses Mirchhouse refused to relinquish their rights, basing the decision on their solicitors' advice. They insisted that a hole should be left in the floor round their seats suitably protected from disaster from the dancers by ropes; as luck would have it the seats were in the back row of the Stalls and consequently on the floor's perimeter, so there was not too much of a problem and, in the event, there is no record of whether the sisters or their nominees ever occupied the seats; perhaps they decided that discretion was the better part of valour because it would seem remarkable, if they had been present, that nobody has left a record of what after all would have been an unusual sight! As for the other seat-holders there appears to have been little objection in spite of the large number involved and they seem to have accepted exclusion from their seats with reasonably good grace though of course they were still allowed free entry to the Hall.

The 1914-18 War led to a major change in financial sponsorship. Unlike the pre-War days, it became the practice for an individual promoter rather then "the Albert Hall" to be responsible for the standard and organisation of events. The return to peacetime conditions also led to demands by the London County Council (L.C.C.) for extensive alterations to be made. Then came the death of the manager, Hilton Carter.

One of his major preoccupations in his last years had been finance, and his thoughts on how future cash could be raised. In a memo on 23rd July 1924, he said that there could be no endowment for working the Hall, which compelled the Administration to seek the aid of Parliament to levy a seat rate which "is far from adequate with increasing rates and charges." The Corporation "is not a trading company, and whatever money is made has to be devoted to the upkeep and improvement" and "for the next three or four years devoted to L.C.C. requirements."

The only financial improvements at this time largely were due to the money obtained from the extra exclusive lettings when the great floor was laid down. By the Act of 1927 the Council's position vis-a-vis the floor was eased when entitlement was granted to erect the floor for up to six weeks at a time if it be deemed "necessary or convenient", though the dispossessed seat-holders still had to be admitted free of charge to the Hall. Financial fortunes soon took a downturn. The borrowing of money was not permissible, but discussion on various ways of raising a loan proved fruitless. One solution was another Act which gave the Corporation power to borrow money. It increased the seat rate liability of seat-holders from £2 per seat per annum to £3. Theatrical entertainments were allowed in the Hall and in various ways the Hall uses were broadened when the great floor was laid.

At about the same time as the Bill was passing through Parliament, Charles Cochran was appointed General Manager, his keenness only being hampered by restrictions on the use of the Hall. He was faced with the problems of getting a Supplemental Charter through the Hall, a matter that was only approved after much argument over the possibility of non seat-holders on the Council. A Select Committee considered the events. As Cochran soon became aware, a tangle of restrictions was imposed by the seat-holders, and unless they were excluded it was difficult to make many apparently likely events pay their way.

In 1934 a new flooring arrangement was purchased, interlocking steel joists replacing the old timber supports. It takes 40 men eight hours to erect, everything having to be hauled up from the basement through trap-doors into the Arena. If the floor is to be used for a dance it is sprung by attaching springs to posts placed into position in special holders; if an exhibition is to be held the posts are capped with collars. This floor has now been in use for nearly half a century and even more than its predecessor has contributed handsomely to the Hall's finances and enormously diversified the scope of activity.

Towards the end of the decade the shadows of the international situation already were stretching over the Hall. A new manager was appointed, Reginald Askew, but he had little to preside over before the last peacetime event took place on 1st July 1939. The Hall was not to reopen until 1941; the main danger as in the First World War being the recognisable glass dome, an easy target for bombers. Quite a few bombs fell nearby, but the building was not hit, though it suffered extensive damage from blast—about 150 large windows and much of the glass in the dome were blown out. First-aid repairs made the building usable and concerts recommenced despite the fact that in 1944 they concided with flying bomb attacks, the audiences courageously ignoring the devilish devices roaring overhead.

In 1943 the Metropolitan Police Commissioner and the Home Secretary and Minister of Home Security banned the use of the Hall at night because if the roof had suffered damage the audience below might well have been endangered.

An aggravation about this time, as pointed out by Myra Hess in a letter to *The Times* in 1943, was that many seat-holders did not notify the Hall of their intended absence, hence many seats remained empty, with consequential financial loss for the many charitable performances.

By 1945, those associated with the Hall were looking to the peace, much as they had done a quarter of a century earlier. Prospects looked bright although there were financial clouds on the horizon, and criticism.

An article in *The Times* in April 1945 hinted at the spirit of a new age arguing that the Hall was unsuitable for any but choral concerts of the old fashioned large-scale kind, and was quite unsuitable for the orchestral music which the public was demanding ever more insistently. Those placed opposite the orchestra heard only the *disjecta membra* of the symphony that was being played, and if it was a piano concerto only the ghost walking in the top Gallery was heard. The side stalls were better but a move to the Boxes changed all the values and criticism becomes little more than guess-work. The acoustics of the building were incurably bad. There were occasions where breadth of effect rather than polished performance sufficed such as big nights at the Proms, and there were certain spectacular shows like the festivals which the Hall could accommodate satisfactorily.

A year later in a *Daily Telegraph* article, Boyd Neel noticed that at the great balls when the dance floor was laid at the level of the First Tier of Boxes, covering the Stalls and Arena, the acoustics were almost perfect. Articles and comments in the press were to occur again the following year.

In October 1947 the question of a ''racket'' in private seats was raised by Sir

The Royal Albert Hall as it approached its centenary, the exterior showing unmistakable effects of the London atmosphere. *Royal Albert Hall*

Adrian Boult, Harold Holt; the Secretary to the Bach Choir, P. Raymond Cooper, and the Chairman of the London Philharmonic Orchestra (L.P.O.), Thomas Russell. They argued that many were in the hands of speculators, and although people could be turned away for events, seats remained empty on the night. The complainants were worried that money for a seat bought for a charity concert would go, not to the charity, but to a ticket agency or the "corner in privately owned seats." An Act of Parliament was necessary to deal with the problem of the propriety of continuing to allow a quarter of the seating capacity of the only full-sized concert hall in London to be governed autonomously by a group of private citizens.

The manager agreed that the large number of seats originally purchased outright for the life of the building had now either passed into the hands of heirs of the original subscribers or in many cases had been sold for profit, and with exception of ten days in the year, proprietary seats had to be kept open by the management of the Hall for their owners.

Seat owners and trustees stung by the implication that they were parasites on the Hall argued that they were the legitimate property owners. Support for this view was given by the President of the Council, the Earl of Lucan, who also stated that the sale of privately owned seats had been greatly exaggerated. He said this was discouraged by the Council and forbidden at the Box Office where every step was taken to protect the promoter's interest. The Corporation had no endowment or subsidy and any profits arising from lettings were applied to the upkeep and improvement of the building. He totally dissociated himself from the views expressed by Dr Herbert Smith that private seats were being sold at a profit for performances and private individuals enjoying entertainments without cost.

These arguments were barely over before concern began to be expressed about the size of the debt encumbering the Hall and the question was raised as to whether it was possible to maintain an ageing memorial building as a private enterprise. Shareholders were told in late 1950 that it might soon be necessary to eliminate private seats and make the Hall eligible for exchequer or municipal

The interior of one of the boxes as it was in 1954. The furnishings show signs of age.
Royal Albert Hall

support. Lease of the Hall site could never be tampered with, even though such restraint may be viewed as mutually disagreeable and lead through bankruptcy to surrender of the lease.

Finance remained a problem exacerbated by legacies of the War years, and such necessary improvements as a new heating installation, a ventilating system and the reconstruction of the inner dome had to be undertaken at a time of high prices and restrictions. The lofty fluted ceiling was constructed of aluminium instead of glass, comprising a main frame and two skins, the lower perforated and backed with rock wool to provide much more efficient heat insulation and sound absorption than the glass dome and end the bad acoustical reputation of the Hall, which had waxed and waned with generations. The cost of this work amounted to £45,000.

Yet within three years, Sir John Wardlaw Milne painted a depressing and alarming picture of the need for £400,000 for repairs and renovation to make the Hall safe and convenient for the public. The estimation of £400,000 was made in respect of long-term reconditioning, the immediate requirement being £240,000.

His fears were to a certain extent alleviated by the 1951 Royal Albert Hall Act which stipulated that seat-holders had to pay a capital contribution of £280 for every seat held, in addition to the seat rate; the borrowing powers of the Corporation rose fourfold to £500,000, and the Council received extra power to exclude seat-holders on 18 days each year. As a result of the Act major repairs were put in hand.

By 1954 it was being argued that as a result of the opening of the Royal Festival Hall in 1951, London now had two major centres, neither of them prospering and one of them a burden to London ratepayers. The previous year the Hall had made a profit of £3,667 and also received a loan of £40,000 interest free from public funds to bolster its fortunes. This came at a time when plans had been on the drawing board for over four years to rebuild the Queen's Hall—a plan not relished by the Council which realised that the B.B.C. would use the new Queen's Hall for its Promenade Concerts.

In 1955 the Hall was placed on the scheduled list of buildings of historic or architectural interest by the Ministry of Housing and Local Government.

A rise in its estimation of architectural value coincided with an increase in its popularity and bookings. Above all, its financial position and prospects were much improved. Such points no doubt were made clear by the President and Vice President of the Council when they held a dinner for newspaper editors and top men of Fleet Street in March 1958. On 3rd June the Duke of Edinburgh attended the 1,000th meeting of the Council. He had been supplied with reports of the Works and Catering Committees, and had three months accounts details to study before attending the meeting. No special dispensations were made and by all accounts the Duke enjoyed the meeting.

This upsurge was contemporaneous with the publication of Ronald Clark's book on the Hall, published at £1. 5s. (£1.25) by Hamish Hamilton in 1958, and widely acclaimed by the critics.

The year 1960 witnessed a new look Hall yet again with improvements completed at a cost of £145,000, including the secondary gas lighting being replaced by a modern emergency lighting system. 11,000 gas mantles were replaced by a new installation of 3,500 electric bulbs. In 1959-60 a permanent orchestral pit was made, so it could be exposed when required or covered to form the normal flooring of the Arena when not in use. It was used for the first time in June 1960 for the visit of the Bolshoi Ballet.

In 1964, the President, Lord Pender, stated that the Hall faced the threat of closure after 93 years of existence because of the financial problems. He warned that orchestral concerts had to be of very high calibre to draw maximum attendances, and the Hall offered no strong appeal to a promoter who knew that 1,287 of the best seats were privately owned and not available for sale at the Box Office. A special sub-committee was trying to get the restricted powers of the Corporation enlarged by Act of Parliament to allow for increasing the number of exclusive lettings, increasing the seat rate and to do things at present not within its powers.

In 1966 it was announced that the private seat-holders would have to pay more to meet increasing competition from subsidised halls. Each paid £10 annually and could be excluded from only 18 events a year at the option of the Council.

Within months an Act of Parliament raised the annual levy payable by seat-holders from £10 to £36, and limited the number of free admissions still further. Yet they still had a bargain and their privileged survival discouraged those who wished to rent the Hall in hope of a profit, and excludes the Hall from access to public funds.

This last item was becoming steadily more serious, if only because the Hall's chief competitor, the Festival Hall, received massive public aid. No Government help has come the way of the Albert Hall since the interest free loan of £40,000 in 1953, a mere drop in the ocean.

The Hall was still attracting larger and larger audiences and the relative appeal of events in the mid '60s makes an interesting study—Concerts—100%; Boxing—95%; Variety and miscellaneous—89%; Wrestling—85%; Jazz—76%; Judo—71%; Other sports—69%; Exhibitions—51%; Arena dances—49%; Youth organisations—42%; Political meetings—29%; Miscellaneous meetings—29%; Religious meetings—28%; Private functions—24%; Reunions—22%; National conferences—22%; International conferences—22%; Learned societies—20%; Prizegivings—12%.

As the Hall approached its hundredth year this was proof enough of versatility.

Mention has already been made of the affairs of the Royal Albert Hall being governed by various Acts of Parliament from its establishment by Royal Charter in 1867 to the most recent legislation in 1966. All major changes in activities and finances come under the close scrutiny of the Palace of Westminster and what is authorised there does not cover all eventualities, far from it. Money matters have always been one of the principal worries of the Council and though the granting of charity status in 1967 brought a measure of relief it also brought the Hall's affairs under the scrutiny of the Charity Commissioners, yet another Crown body. So it is that the running of the Hall is strictly controlled and limited and the Council has to operate within those limitations, a task which never seems to have been easy at any time during the Hall's long and eventful history.

By the time the centenary celebrations were approaching it was realised that something should be done to modernise, clean and refurbish the building but the problem was the raising of the necessary finance. As the Hall has no endowment its running costs have to be obtained by letting, profits from the Catering Department and the annual subscriptions of the 363 seatholders who between them own 1,287 of the 5,606 seats. As personal property they can be bought and sold and devolved by will and many of the present holders are descendants of the original purchasers of a century and more ago. The money raised from these sources provided nothing towards the cost of the work contemplated in the early 1970s so the Council decided to launch a national appeal in February 1970 for half a million pounds; this was as a result of a suggestion by Frank Mundy who had been appointed General Manager in 1966 and directly led to the application for charity status and the financial advantages that would result if it was accepted. An appeal for money on this scale would have been unlikely to have achieved success if the backing of a group of well known personalities had not been obtained to supply a flourish and give an encouraging start to the project. Happily there was little difficulty in getting men and women of goodwill to lend their names as sponsors of the appeal and they represented a wide cross section of interests and talents, including church and state, local government, the services, law, stage and screen, music, banking, science, industry, entertainment, the media and many others.

As a preliminary to the cleaning and restoration it was decided once and for all to settle the acoustical problem that had bedevilled the Hall right from the start. In 1968 the Acoustical Investigation Research Organisation was appointed and carried out various recordings and tests over a period of many months from stations in different parts of the Hall. A considerable amount of information on echoes and reverberations was gleaned from these exhaustive tests and with the aid of the Building Research Station at Garston in Hertfordshire a solution was found that resulted in almost the complete elimination of the problem. An arrangement of 135 fibreglass rigid mouldings in the shape of inverted domes, which became euphemistically known as 'flying saucers' after the space objects allegedly seen by many people about that time, were suspended from 360 individual points and filled with glassfibre wool; in total they covered an area of some 10,000 sq. ft. and were in position by the summer of 1969. In addition it was found to be necessary to replace the ancient valarium which had been a dust trap for so many years. The valarium's replacement was a modification of the "saucers" into three reflector elements, each of which was 12 feet deep from back to front; the element nearest the organ is 42 feet long, the centre one 4 feet longer and the outermost one a further 4 feet longer, giving a maximum length of 50 feet. Twelve years later the "saucers" and orchestra reflector are still giving satisfactory service and have become quite a feature of the Hall. The cost of £8,000 was shared by the Arts Council and the B.B.C.

By the time the centenary concert was given on 29th March 1971 the main entrance porch had been enclosed to give protection from the weather for members of the public waiting to enter the Hall and a large renovated and resplendent Victorian gasolier, suitably converted to electricity, installed. The repair of the exterior had been completed apart from some non urgent work to the roof and, with help from the Historic Buildings Council, the accumulated grime of a century removed from the walls by the low pressure wet grit blast method. The foyer, corridors and main staircases were re-decorated to designs by Sir Hugh and Lady Casson in a two-tone scheme of golden-ochre and red for the walls, white ceilings and black doors and skirtings with gold sign-writing and prismatic light fittings. Scarlet velvet curtains were hung in the tiered boxes and the occasional chairs in them stained black and melamine covered drop leaf tables provided. Areas subject to especially hard wear were covered with black and red marbled rubber and those less prone to the tramp of marching feet were provided with black and scarlet carpeting designed by Joyce Conwy Evans; radiators were enclosed and even new signs and ashtrays provided. At the end of 1972 the original financial objective was £93,000 short of being achieved and at the same time it was revealed that inflation had added 40% to the target figure, raising the sum required to £700,000. It immediately became obvious that such an amount was unlikely to be reached unaided by the appeal fund so the Council President, Sir Louis Gluckstein, approached the Paymaster General, who was the Minister responsible for the Arts, and in February, 1973 it was announced that the Government would match pound for pound up to a limit of £150,000 the money which the appeal could raise by the end of March, 1974. No only was the sum raised on time but two special donations were received that finally put the financial minds at rest; £100,000 was given by the Bernard Sunley Charitable Foundation and £50,000 by the Greater London Council. In addition the Charles Hayward Foundation provided an invalid and handicapped persons lift and the organ was renovated and modernised at a cost of £27,000, largely donated by Mrs Sue Hammerson.

The Balcony Restaurant, formerly the theatre. *Royal Albert Hall*

As the money came in so did the improvements and restoration proceed; new goods and platform lifts and platform lighting were installed, improvements made to the kitchens and toilets, the curtaining, carpeting and other floor covering was completed, the stalls seating renewed, and the re-decoration finished. Most of the work was executed whilst the Hall remained open and caused considerable inconvenience and additional expenditure; wherever possible mobile equipment was used and had to be moved prior to each evenings' events and then put back into position the following morning. Daytime events impeded progress though work frequently continued during rehearsals but even so the Hall finally had to be closed for five weeks during the summer of 1974 in order that everything could be finished in time for the season of Promenade Concerts. Sadly Frank Mundy died suddenly in February of that year and so did not live to enjoy the fulfilment of that which he had striven so long and hard to accomplish.

More recently, in 1977, the latest renovations have been completed though these are not apparent to the general public since they have encompassed the modernisation of the various rooms used by conductors, artistes and choirs; most of their users would agree this was a long overdue transformation to bring amenities up to the standard expected of a principal concert hall of one of the great cities of the world.

After the Hall was designated a listed building, special problems were posed for those involved in the alterations and renovations, but these were successfully surmounted by the architects, designers and contractors and the finished product bears testimony to their skill and taste. The architects, Ronald Ward & Partners, received a Civic Trust Award in 1973, and then in 1975 a European Architectural Heritage Year Award as did Sir Louis Gluckstein, Sir Hugh Casson, John Laing & Sons Ltd., and Holloway White Allom Ltd., the painting contractors.

Apart from the modernising and refurbishing of the building a particularly attractive way of commemorating the Hall's centenary in 1971 was the idea of

A Wedgwood Blue Jasper sweet dish produced to commemorate the centenary of the Hall.
Josiah Wedgwood and Sons

having a new rose named after the famous building. The well known specialists, James Cocker & Sons Ltd., of Aberdeen, were approached and readily agreed to oblige, the result being advertised for the first time in their 1972-3 catalogue. This beautiful creation is a Hybrid Tea with a height of 2-2½ feet and described as "very fragrant" with a parentage of Fragrant Cloud X Postillon.

Another centenary commemorative idea was the production of a Wedgwood Blue Jasper sweet dish with a representation of the Hall in the centre; also a similar trinket box with the Hall on the lid.

Sir Louis Gluckstein referred in 1971 to a million visitors a year going to the Hall and anyone can see for themselves the public parts of the building. This can be done by merely purchasing a ticket for a concert, meeting, sporting event, festive occasion or whatever, just as has been possible for a century or more. Much of both inside and outside has already been described in previous chapters but there are of course the more private parts of the building which the man in the street is not privileged to witness.

For most people the principal obscurities are probably the Royal Box and Retiring Room. Contrary to what many believe the former is not used exclusively by the Royal Family and when not in such use the seats are offered to members of the Royal household who frequently take advantage of this privilege. When members of the Royal Family are expected the normal red furnishings are changed; a royal blue carpet is laid, gold velvet curtains are hung, blue or pink covered chairs brought in and, to complete the transformation, a gold and crimson, fringed and tasselled, turquoise blue velvet hanging with the Royal coat of arms embossed in gold is draped over the front of the Box. A rather peculiar anomaly in present circumstances is the crown facing onto the Auditorium above the Royal Box; this is a King's crown put up to replace the Queen's crown stolen at a Bomber Command Reunion on 19th May 1950.

The Royal Retiring Room is at the rear of the Box, across the corridor which is closed to usage by the public when Royalty is present by the drawing of a curtain. The room walls are covered with oyster moiré silk with matching curtains; there is a blue carpet, the furnishings are in gilt with red damask coverings and the whole is illuminated by a fine crystal chandelier and wall sconces. On a side table are bronze heads of Victoria and Albert, made in 1862 by William Theed, and round the walls are gilt framed etchings of British monarchs and their consorts from Victoria to George VI. Queen Elizabeth and Prince Philip are represented by photographs, that of Her Majesty being signed personally when she visited the Hall for the centenary celebrations on 29th March 1971.

On the opposite side of the Grand Tier to the Royal Box there are three rooms named after men who did so much to bring the Hall into existence—the Prince Consort, General Scott and Henry Cole. All are used for private functions, the two latter being suitable for only the smallest of gatherings. The Prince Consort Room is considerably larger than the other two rooms and is used from time to time for official receptions. An interesting feature are the original drawings used in the construction of the mosaic frieze high up on the Hall's external wall; they are the only formation planning details in the Hall's possession, all the rest being in the keeping of the Greater London Council (G.L.C.). Adjoining the Henry Cole Room is the Council Room, the regular meeting place of Council members for discussion, decision making and luncheons, to which the Queen and Queen Mother were entertained respectively on 30th October 1974 and 6th May 1976.

The artistes' and conductors' rooms have the red carpeting synonymous with the rest of the building and are supplied with comfortable but not lavish easy chairs and settees covered in checked tweed material. Being situated in the basement there is no natural lighting so illumination is provided by wall sconces and, in the case of the artistes' rooms, by strip lights over rows of dressing tables. At an even lower level are the changing rooms for members of choirs and orchestras which are also used by those taking part in pageants or other events requiring costume change. All these rooms are adequately provided with toilet facilities, including showers; this was not always the case, however, and leading performers between the two World Wars were provided with a bath by the stokers who had acquired it to cleanse themselves when they came off duty in the boiler house. The ''also ran'' performers did not qualify for such luxury and had to be content to await their turn to use the meagre and primitive facilities available or else bravely travel home still adorned in their make-up.

Also occupying the basement are the boiler house, kitchens and wine cellars. The former somewhat resembles a ship's engine room with its four giant boilers and masses of pipes, wires and gauges. The present gas-fired boilers have been in position since 1949 and can reach full capacity in 20 minutes, a useful attribute considering the vast space that requires warming-up. An improbable sight to the South West of the Hall is a tall brick chimney stack standing on an island in the roadway; this is the discharge outlet for the powerful monsters in the boiler house and its isolation has meant that the elliptical symmetry of the Hall has not been marred by a necessary but ugly excrescence. The huge Victorian kitchens have recently been modernised, thanks to the centenary appeal providing the necessary financial requirements; they now possess all the necessary aids for the provision of high class and speedy catering, attributes of the first order where many different types of function have to be accommodated, many of them in limited periods of time. The Balcony Restaurant, the several Private Rooms, the Boxes and the 10 Bar Buffets, to say nothing of the Royal Retiring Room, all require attention though rarely at the same time. The Restaurant of necessity can only be opened for a series of activities such as the Promenade Concerts or when it is specifically required for wedding or other receptions or business gatherings; the Private Rooms are of course also used for similar occasions and present like problems. Good food requires good serving and presentation and this is provided for by ample stocks of glass, crockery, cutlery and linen which would not disgrace the best of hotels. High class catering in cellar kitchens is all very well but to remain high class all the way to the table is a top priority and is successfully accomplished by rapid handling and speedy service lifts.

Liquid refreshment is also of great importance and the Restaurant and Refreshment Rooms have permanent Bars whilst facilities are provided in the

The Royal Box with the velvet hanging bearing the Royal Arms used when members of the Royal Family are present. *Royal Albert Hall*

DIEU ET MON DROIT

Royal Retiring and Private Rooms when required. The wine cellars are stocked with thousands of bottles of beer, wines, spirits and soft drinks all kept at the correct temperatures to ensure perfection.

The B.B.C. has of course long been established at the Hall and there is now close liaison and harmony between the Corporation and the Hall's Council and management but this has not always been the case. In the spring of 1923 the well known promoters, Chappell & Co., held a meeting attended by agents, artistes and hall managers concerned with the promotion of musical concerts; their first priorities were naturally financial considerations and it is not surprising that a resolution was adopted to the effect that ''the broadcasting of music from places of public entertainment is prejudicial to the interests of all connected with such places'' and all present were asked to reject the blandishments of the B.B.C. The Council's response was immediate and Chappell's were notified ''that there is no intention under present circumstances, on the part of the Council of the Royal Albert Hall, to allow the Hall to be used for the purpose of broadcasting.'' The ''present circumstances'' were, however, not destined to endure for very long because a bare 15 months later the Council reversed its decision, albeit with some qualification. On 22nd July 1924 it was resolved ''that the Royal Choral Society may have the right to broadcast their concerts on the condition that the consent of the various soloists, orchestras and conductors, in writing, is previously obtained''. These few words were sufficient to open the door and on 20th December that same year the Society's annual carol concert was the first ever broadcast from the Hall. The second broadcast followed on 9th March 1925 with the B.B.C. promoting a Community Singing Concert; the following year the Corporation paid the Hall £800 for broadcasting 12 concerts and so the long association of the two bodies got well and truly under way. In the early days the control point and mixing facilities were situated beneath the

platform, the microphones being slung on wires suspended across the Hall at Balcony level, from whence the sound was transmitted by landline to Savoy Hill.

By the 1940s more congenial circumstances prevailed for the B.B.C. and the announcers had advanced to being installed in one of the Loggia Boxes where they could see what they were supposed to be talking about. Mixing was transferred from the nether regions of the platform to the nether regions of one of the entrance staircases, where it must have been difficult since it was only six feet wide. Savoy Hill had long ceased to be the Corporation's home and the relays were now landlined to Broadcasting House in Portland Place. 1942 was the year of further advances in broadcasting technique and many experiments were made with regard to microphone sitings both then and in subsequent years. At first the Hall's infamous echo was eliminated but the resulting performances as they came over the air were acoustically "dead" and had to be revitalised by the use of what was euphemistically described as an "echo room" from which reverberation was added to the sound produced. Eventually as a result of re-positioning the orchestral players and considerable juggling around with the microphone placements the broadcast sound was enormously improved. The mixing room was moved yet again, first to Loggia Box No. 2 and then way up to a room on the Balcony. The commentary positions occupy two sound-proofed Loggia Boxes and can accommodate up to three commentators serving as many different programmes if necessary. The permanent facilities now comprise six microphone points underneath the platform, four on the platform and seven on the Balcony, though additional points can be added as and when required for particular events.

Television technicians regard the Hall as the most popular place in London for outside studio broadcasts. The number of cameras varies from 12 for the Miss World contest to five for the Proms (two on stage, two in the Grand Tier and

Opposite: The Royal Albert Hall kitchen in the 1940s.

Right: The Prince Consort Suite. *Royal Albert Hall*

Television in the Hall: the Eurovision Song Contest held on 6th April 1968. *Royal Albert Hall*

one in the Gallery). For concerts, a hand held camera is concealed in the artistes' stage entry passage (known to the staff as the "bull run") to obtain views as seen by the players. Although skeletal equipment remains as a permanent feature, the lighting is moved in and out of the Hall as required. Lighting is the most costly element and is organised by the B.B.C. engineers in collaboration with the Hall. Both radio and televison have been provided with permanent facilities in the shape of cabling which only requires a "plug-in" to function. The cameras send their pictures to a scanner vehicle parked outside which relays the signals to the Television Centre from whence it goes to a transmitting mast at Crystal Palace.

It may be wondered how an announcer sitting in the Auditorium can foresee the imminent arrival of the leader and conductor of an orchestra and an artiste or artistes on the platform before their actual appearance; and also how the performers know when the announcer has completed the introductory remarks to the concert and they are able to make their appearance. Such co-ordination is carried out by means of a telephone link between the announcer and a B.B.C. staff member manning the instrument situated outside the rooms used by the performers; with which he is in contact by means of a set of indicator lights.

Broadcasting and televising are now commonplace activities at the Hall but what is considerably rarer is film making, though this has certainly occurred, scenes having been shot for the Alfred Hitchcock thriller *The Man Who Knew Too Much* starring Doris Day and James Stewart; Italian film makers have also practised their art in the precincts.

On passing through the main entrance into the foyer the visitor will notice on the facing wall not only the plaque unveiled by the Queen to mark the Hall's centenary but also a clock given by the Corps of Honorary Stewards to mark the same occasion and a modern portrait of one of England's greatest, but perhaps least understood, composers, Frederick Delius, presented by the Council. There are also busts and portraits of Victoria and Albert as reminders of the Hall's historical past and even its origins; indeed Albert cannot readily be avoided since the "A" motif appears in many places, even on the balusters of the staircase leading up to the Royal Retiring Room. Other mementos of long ago are the original night watchman's clock, a collection of keys, including an unusual double one, used by private box owners, a centenary medal and the original programme for the opening of the Hall; all these are kept secure in the General Manager's office along with the other treasures mentioned in an earlier chapter.

Successful operation of an enterprise as large, complex and diversified as the Royal Albert Hall requires expert guidance at the top and dedicated men and women to carry out expertly and conscientiously the day-to-day duties that keep the wheels running smoothly. The Council is, as we have already seen, elected annually from members of the Corporation, that is those who are seat owners, and is liable for general policy making and overall administration, meeting at frequent and regular intervals to carry out its reponsibilities. In addition to the elected members there are appointee members representing respectively the British Museum, Natural History, the Chancellor of the Duchy of Lancaster, the Imperial College of Science and Technology, the Royal College of Music and the Royal Commissioners for the Exhibition of 1851; these appointments are to comply with the conditions of the Supplemental Charter of 1928. In the case of the three last named the appointed member has to be a member of the appointing body. The five appointee members and the 18 elected members are chaired by a President so that the total complement of the Council is 24.

The day-to-day administration of the Hall is in the hands of a General Manager assisted by a Technical Services Manager, an Assistant General Manager, a Secretary and Lettings Manager, a Box Office Manager whose staff handles more than a million tickets per annum, a Catering Manager and a Chief Accountant; all are supported by various assistants and secretaries. Then there is a Hall Superintendent and his deputy, the Foreman of Works, responsible for the general maintenance of the building and for all technical arrangements required by individual promoters. To assist them in their multifarious duties there are carpenters, heating and ventilating personnel, electricians, firemen, who maintain a round-the-clock watch, a glazier, a rigger and even an upholsterer, who on average deals with two of the seats every day. The Hall Superintendent shares the duty of attendance at all functions with the General and Assistant General Managers and three other persons, including the Lettings Manager and the Catering Manager. The senior managers share the responsibility of general administrative duties. Other staff include the Housekeeper, the switchboard, tannoy and bleeping systems' operators, the Commissionaires, the Artistes' Door Attendant, who usually gets a friendly greeting from the famous as they enter and leave, the Backstage Attendant who looks after the artistes' requirements, the Attendants who look after the patrons in the Boxes, the army of cleaners and the many casual staff who are so often called upon to help out on the big occasions. Changes in staff organisation are currently under way.

To usher an audience of several thousands through thirteen entrances into as many blocks of seating in a very limited space of time, perhaps half an hour at most, requires more than a modicum of patience, tact and firmness. When it is considered that those that carry out these stewarding duties receive as their only reward two tickets in specially reserved boxes, and these only when the steward himself is on duty, it is perhaps remarkable that the Corps of Stewards has survived for well over a century.

Stewarding of some sort was of course a necessity right from the earliest days and in fact dates from the Hall's opening when the Provisional Committee approached the Sacred Harmonic Society with a request that it might provide from its membership stewards to supervise the smooth seating and dispersal of the great concourse expected to assemble. The Society was accustomed to stewarding its own concerts at Exeter Hall and was going to provide the chorus for the important ceremony so perhaps it was the most logical of bodies to approach when as many as 150 men were required to ensure the smooth running of the illustrious Royal occasion. As the reward for volunteering was a free admission ticket it is not surprising that there was little difficulty in recruiting the requisite number to be on duty on the great day. Apparently one and all performed satisfactorily because the Society was asked three weeks later to officiate at the first International Exhibition and thereafter at its own series of concerts held in the Summer. From this rather haphazard beginning the Corps of Honorary Stewards evolved and could, therefore, be said to be as old as the Hall itself, developing and expanding over the years an aura and tradition of its own; there is little doubt that it is unique, there being virtual certainty that it has no counterpart anywhere else in the world. In 1931 rules for members stated that failure to make three consecutive attendances make the offender liable to have his name removed from the roll. Eight years later, 60% of attendances were made obligatory. In 1942 the Council reorganised the Corps into what is practically a semi-autonomous body with its own Constitution and administration vested in two Superintendents and two assistants. It is their responsibility to detail each member's duty dates and positions within the Hall and this can frequently raise problems connected with the business and personal commitments of each individual which may have the effect of leaving too many stewards available on some occasions and too few on others.

Members of the Corps, who have their own room in the depths of the Hall close to the artistes', conductors' and dressing rooms, represent a wide cross section of the public, many being retired and therefore getting on in years, whilst those still active in their occupations are drawn from the professions, the services, commerce and industry. At present the complement is about 70 and their badge of office is the monogram RAH surmounted by a crown in silver and worn in the lapel. Each event requires at least 30 of the Corps to be on duty so approximately half the members are present at every event which means all are subject to frequent calls upon their services; they cannot pick and choose to serve only on those occasions which particularly interest them and they have to agree to this condition upon joining the Corps. As many as 30 events may be held each month in the Hall and anywhere between 250 and 300 in a year so the Superintendents and their assistants have quite a problem on their hands trying to accommodate their fellow members and at the same time ensuring that the needs of the Hall are adequately covered. Initially stewards have to serve throughout the Hall, but then they move to a permanent position, starting with the Balcony and ending after years of service at the entrance. Their duties are not just the mundane like showing people to the correct seats but acting with a due sense of decorum to those that arrive late for performances and resent being thwarted in their efforts to take their seats until a convenient moment arrives that will cause least annoyance to those who arrived on time; then there is the

The Box Office just after the Second World War. *Royal Albert Hall*

occasional double booking of seats to sort out, frequently with only minutes to spare before the performance commences and the innumerable questions about the Hall to answer, often asked by foreigners with limited understanding of English. Nearly all the stewards have one prime interest—music, mainly of a classical type. Relations with the Council and the Hall Management have been most cordial—members were presented to the Queen during the centenary year of 1971, and in November 1980 the Superintendents and Assistant Super-

Queen Elizabeth II unveiling a plaque to commemorate the centenary of the opening of the Hall.
Royal Albert Hall

intendents were invited to lunch with the Council at their monthly meeting, in appreciation of the work by members of the Corps.

The Lettings Manager, as the name implies, is responsible for the Hall's bookings which involves working as much as two years in advance and requires consummate tact and more than a modicum of diplomacy in order to keep the many promoters of events sweet and in good humour; this accomplishment is not always easy to achieve when different promoters and organisations clamour for conflicting dates. Certain events are, however, easy to slot into the lettings calendar as, like the Festival of Remembrance, they are held always at accustomed times.

As each event comes round tickets for it have to be printed and sold; the printing process was at one time carried out on the premises but since 1947 an outside firm has been employed to do this. Before printing can commence, however, the promoter of an event has to decide on the price he wants to charge for seats in different parts of the Hall, based on the gross takings he hopes to receive—a difficult assessment to make since he is unaware how the public will react to his bill of fare by filling the Hall to capacity or otherwise. In this tricky business he can call on the services of the Deputy Manager for advice. Sometimes decisions are easy to come by such as when a famous overseas orchestra directed by an internationally known conductor is due to appear; then it is a safe assumption that there will be a complete "sell-out" but events that are likely to produce less than capacity audiences are much more difficult to assess in financial terms. However, the long experience accumulated by the Hall more often than not comes up with answers that ultimately prove to be remarkably accurate. When the tickets are received at the Box Office they are checked to make sure all are there and correctly numbered and then those for the privately held seats are extracted and despatched to the holders. All then is clear for the sale of those that remain by the full time staff of ten and casuals employed as and when required. These people have to cope with personal, postal and telephone bookings, possibly for up to 30 events at a time, frequently with different prices for each. Things get worse as the booking opens for the Promenade Concert Season because 50 concerts have tickets on sale concurrently.

To provide adequate catering facilities for a daily attendance of many thousands of patrons, often split into afternoon and evening audiences and also for those taking part in rehearsals and subsequent performances is a tremendous task. Highly sophisticated menus can be served as well as the simplest of sandwiches or specialised confections such as wedding cakes and personalised tributes for anniversaries, presentations and such like. It is perhaps fair to say, however, that the more routine requirement is the production of snacks such as sandwiches, rolls, cakes, pastries and biscuits but even on this scale the feeding of thousands is formidable indeed especially as availability has to be ensured before and after the event and in the interval as well. There are other occasions when far more is called for and a full catering requirement of "set table" places and several course menus is a proposition for cool heads and strong nerves. Large and varied amounts of drink are required to go with, or even without, the food and many thousands of pounds worth can be disposed of in the ten bars at each event. The serving of both food and drink in very short periods of time is a problem in itself but, coupled with the preparation, the clearing away and the washing-up, is a task calling for considerable organising ability and dedication by the kitchen and bar staffs. In these respects the Catering Manager and his Deputy are assisted by a Chef de Cuisine and six cooks, a Head Cellarman and Head Barman with innumerable permanent and casual staff and there are certainly no passengers when it is remembered that the feeding and drinking points are scattered all over the building, that up to 1,400 may sit down to dinner in the Arena, plus those doing likewise in the Boxes and Stalls; or alternatively full buffet service has to be provided in the Boxes and Gallery when a dance is in progress.

The Hall Superintendent and Foreman of Works with a permanent staff of over 20 control security arrangements and have the job of switching the amenities and facilities to suit the wide range of events that the Hall hosts in a year, ranging from the large number of concerts, to political and religious meetings, from dances to sporting occasions and from festivals to reunions and conferences. All these multifarious activities require such things as special lighting, flooring, staging and seating arrangements and the whole place is regularly turned upside down and back again to accommodate all the different combinations that such events require. If a dance is due to take place all the seats in the Arena have to be removed into the basement before the special floor can be laid by outside contractors, a process of several hours duration. Other outside contractors are responsible for any additional lighting requirements that promoters might require for their events and this is installed under the overall supervision of the Chief Electrician, as stringent precautions are taken to prevent the possibility of a fire occurring, this being the immediate responsibility of the Chief Fireman. Cleaning up after each event is controlled by the Housekeeper and is a considerable task in itself because, like so many other things in the day-to-day running of the Hall, time is the essence; in this respect the Housekeeper relies not only on members of the Superintendent's staff but also on casual employees. In addition to all these wide ranging activities the Hall's general maintenance comes under the aegis of the Superintendent and to this end he is assisted by staff skilled in different building trades so that he is not constantly in need of calling in outsiders to carry out routine carpentry, joinery, plumbing and the like.

The Chief Accountant's responsibilities include the financial settlements with all the individual promoters, the payment of salaries and wages of the 110 permanent and host of casual employees, including the associated ramifications of insurance and taxation; also the settlement of all accounts received in respect of goods and services rendered and the voluminous amount of work raised by the operations of the catering department in the kitchens, bars and restaurant for both public and private functions.

A recent innovation occurred in March 1981 with the opening of a Souvenir Shop in the foyer of Door 9. Its contents include memorabilia to do with the Hall and its functions and London life of particular interest to tourists.

The Royal Albert Hall caters for a wider range of artistic, social and sporting events than any other in the whole of the United Kingdom and its capacity of three and a half million cubic feet is often taxed to the limit but thanks to the marvellous team spirit generated by all members of staff and the Corps of Honorary Stewards it would seem that its reputation and standing in the life of the community is well assured as it marches onwards to its second century.

CHAPTER FOUR

A Giant Within a Giant

DOMINATING the southern side of the Hall behind the platform is the splendid panoply of the great organ towering impressively above the auditorium to a height of 70 feet. Only five feet less in width, it is one of the largest instruments in the world with four manuals, 176 draw stops and 10,491 speaking pipes which range in length from $\frac{3}{8}$ of an inch to 42 feet, the latter weighing almost a ton. Out of this forest of pipes can be conjured an enormous dynamic range, from a barely audible whisper to a mighty roar fit to shake the very foundations of the building and be acceptable only in the smallest doses by most listeners. There is a relative absence of casing, a mere three ornamental arches supported by side columns with a horizontal traceried band at high level, all gilded to match the Hall's general decor.

"The largest and most complete instrument in the world" was the ambitious reference made to it, though not without due cause, when the Hall was opened and Dr William Thomas Best, at that time organist of St George's Hall, Liverpool, demonstrated the instrument's paces for the first time in public, aided and abetted by motive power obtained from two steam-engines, one of 8 h.p. and the other of 13 h.p. placed next to the bellows-chamber. Though not quite complete for the occasion its merits were finally confirmed when Dr Best gave the inaugural recital on the 18th July of the same year and critics and public alike proclaimed its qualities.

The man entrusted with the building of this mighty instrument was the prince of organ builders of the Victorian era, Henry Willis, who was 16 years old when the Queen came to the throne and died at the age of 80 in the same year that she passed into history. Two years before the Queen's accession Willis was apprenticed to John Gray whose family had been in the organ building business for over 60 years and thus could safely be guaranteed to give the boy a good solid grounding in his chosen vocation.

Willis was not only a scientific organ builder with a thorough understanding of the engineering techniques involved but also a player of some distinction, being for many years the organist of Hampstead Parish Church, playing on an instrument of his own construction. Having started his own business in the 1840s in London's Grays Inn Road, moving some 20 years later to Royal College Street, he was in the obvious and satisfactory position of being selected to build the giant in Albert's great Hall. It was soon followed by the St

Paul's Cathedral instrument and the massive creation in Alexandra Palace, now alas a mass of ashes and twisted metal. Indeed so prolific a builder was "Father" Willis, as he was affectionately known, that in London alone he was responsible for the construction of over 200 instruments.

In spite of Willis' great expertise it was soon apparent to some that for a Hall with a volume of over three million cubic feet the sound was on the thin side though Willis could hardly be blamed for this since nobody before had built an organ for a Hall of such vast proportions. However, sooner or later the pedants had to be appeased and in 1924 the famous Durham firm of Harrison & Harrison were commissioned to rebuild the instrument in two stages in order to spread the financial burden, the work being completed in 1933. On submitting the firm's complete reconstruction scheme at an estimated cost of £25,000 in January of the previous year Arthur Harrison had this to say in his report to the Council—"We consider it an instrument of superb construction and a monument to the skill of its builder, the late Henry Willis . . . We think it will be agreed that any work of restoration and improvement should be approached in a spirit similar to that which actuated the original builder and should be carried out with equal thoroughness."

A somewhat curious usage of the instrument after the first stage of the restoration in the late 1920s was during boxing bouts and these occasions prompted Sir Hugh Allen, the director of the Royal College of Music, to comment that the organ "is worthy of a better fate than that of being something used for drowning noises at boxing matches." *The Musical Times* of December 1926 quoted from a newspaper report of a fight that "The organ at the Albert Hall, London, which has proved useful during boxing contests, was once more played with considerable force last night to drown the sustained booing that greeted the referee's verdict . . ."

Further restoration to the action motors and blowing apparatus took place in the mid 1950s and a humidifying plant was installed to overcome the dry atmospheric effects resulting from modern central heating methods. In the early 1960s the pitch was raised to the standard at 65°F (18°C) for C, namely 523.3 vibrations. Finally in 1973 the console underwent major surgery by which it received new keys, pedal board and piston layout and at the same time the pneumatic parts of the coupler and combination actions were converted to a solid-state system, thereby outdating the humidifier installed 20 years previously. The effect of this work, spread over nearly 50 years, has been to virtually create a new instrument though most of the old pipes were reused after rescaling and revoicing. New stops were added to the original number of 111 to increase the instrument's range and versatility and the remodelling and renovation has been so extensive that what was once a Willis organ has now become a Harrison organ, none the worse for that but perhaps somewhat regrettable that the original connection with Willis and his Victorian patrons has largely disappeared. Harrison & Harrison, like Willis, have a highly distinguished reputation and examples of their work are to be found in the Royal Festival Hall, the Fairfield Halls, Croydon, and the Colston Hall, Bristol, apart from such cathedrals as those of Coventry, Durham, Ely, Lincoln, Wells, Winchester and Worcester, not forgetting Westminster Abbey and King's College Chapel, Cambridge. So one of the master organ builders of the 19th century has been succeeded by one of the 20th century and between them for well over a hundred years they have ensured that the Royal Albert Hall has had an instrument worthy of its world wide prestige and renown. So much so that the Hall's manager during the Second World War, Charles Taylor, is quoted as saying, "I got so many requests from American soldiers for permission to play the organ that I began to suspect that the Army had been recruited almost exclusively from organists."

Dr Leo L. Beranek, the American acoustical consultant, said after listening to a performance of Tchaikovsky's Overture, *1812*: "The great organ sounded like the voice of Jupiter. The audience was left breathless and tingling. It is for these moments of ecstasy that the Albert Hall continues to exist." On the other hand the organ is equally capable of producing exquisite sounds at the opposite

Sir George Thalben-Ball, curator of the Great Organ since 1934. *Lauri Tjurin*

end of the voice spectrum—upper register strings and woodwind—so the instrument is superbly balanced to perform the widest possible range of musical sound. Perhaps the end result has justified the means but there are probably many who regret the 1921 decision to place the restoration work in the hands of others than the successors of "Father" Willis, who were available and no doubt would have more than justified their appointment.

A fine instrument requires a fine exponent to adequately demonstrate its qualities and in this respect the Royal Albert Hall has been fortunate indeed. Mention has already been made of Dr Best playing at the Hall's opening ceremony and giving the inaugural concert. Prior to being appointed the Hall's first official organist he had been at Liverpool for seventeen years and was therefore well versed in the playing of a large instrument and he was destined to hold the dual appointment until 1894. He was born in Carlisle in 1826 and died in Liverpool in 1897. Regarded as the greatest concert organist of the 19th century, he could well be considered the first such that England ever possessed; he had an enormous repertoire, not only performing all the classic organ music but large quantities of orchestral and other music which he arranged himself for the organ. He also composed works for the instrument as well as Church music and published an edition of Handel's organ works. In 1934 George Thalben-Ball was appointed organist and curator, a post he still occupies in 1982. On 23rd January 1934 he was one of the trio of organists, Sir Walter Alcock of Salisbury Cathedral and G. D. Cunningham of Birmingham Town Hall being the others, who recommissioned the organ after its major reconstruction by Harrison and Harrison.

Thalben-Ball had made his reputation at the Temple Church where in 1919 he was appointed Organist and Choir Director and in 1949 he became Birmingham City and University Organist. On 27th September 1979 David & Charles published Jonathan Rennert's biography of the Doctor and to underline this event he gave a private recital for some of his friends followed by a reception in the Prince Consort Room. He received a knighthood in 1982.

Very many guest artistes have over the years performed at the console, amongst the first being no less a person than the famous Austrian composer and Court Organist at Vienna, Anton Bruckner, who appeared on the 2nd August, just four months after the Hall was opened. Other famous instrumentalists include Jennifer Bate, Ralph Davier, Reginald Dixon, Marcel Dupré, Reginald Foort, Alan Foster, Fernando Germani, Nicolas Kynaston, Jean Langlais, Quentin Maclean, Jane Parker-Smith, Flor Peeters, Simon Preston, Alexander Schreiner and Gillian Weir; several of them have made recordings in the Hall either as soloists or in the performance of choral and orchestral works and there is little doubt that now the Hall is well on its way towards its second century its musical giant will remain as popular as ever with performer and public alike.

CHAPTER FIVE

The Promenade Concerts

THE 10th May 1941 witnessed one of the greatest and most destructive of the wartime fire raids on London; as a result one of the many things the capital lost was the home for nearly 46 years of the famous Henry Wood Promenade Concerts.

The Promenade Concerts had started in August 1895 in the Queen's Hall, Langham Place, next to All Souls Church where the St George's Hotel now stands. They were destined to continue without interruption through all the crises of war and peace until that fateful night of the Second World War. When war was declared on 3rd September, the 1939 season of Proms had been in progress for three weeks and they came to an abrupt halt with the evacuation to Bedford of the B.B.C. Symphony Orchestra. Air raids were expected daily and it was generally considered that there was little if any chance of the Proms being resumed until hostilities ceased. Such pessimism was quickly dispelled because by the time the 1940 season came round salvation was at hand.

Keith Douglas was at the time Honorary Secretary of the Royal Philharmonic Society and he decided that the Proms, the last one at Queen's Hall having been on 7th September 1940, should not be allowed to lapse, war or no war. He engaged the London Symphony Orchestra (L.S.O.) with Sir Henry Wood as principal conductor and Basil Cameron as his associate, but the series was not destined to achieve completion because in September the concerts were abandoned when the main blitz developed. Then followed the destructive events of May 1941 and the transfer by Douglas of the concerts to the Royal Albert Hall. A strange irony that the removal from the London scene of a hall, which at its inception was going to be named either Victoria or Queen's, should be succeeded as the home of the Proms by the Hall named after and in memory of Her Majesty's late husband. Ironic also that in the Summer of 1915 Sir Thomas Beecham and Sir Landon Ronald should have attempted to run a rival series of Proms in the Royal Albert Hall, only to fail miserably because the audiences did not justify the means even though the series was given an unqualified compliment at the end by the *Musical Times* which referred to it as "one of the most admirable ever given in London." The Proms meant Queen's Hall and Wood, and Queen's Hall and Wood meant the Proms and that was that; at least until force of circumstances changed the picture and broke the synonymity.

Douglas, who had booked the Royal Albert Hall the day after the destruction of Queen's Hall, made his first objective before a note was played to do something about the Hall's acoustics which were still giving cause for concern and irritation; as Beecham once said, "It is invaluable for those who are slow on the musical uptake—they hear everything three times. And it is the only place in which some composers are likely to hear more than one performance of their works." At another time he remarked facetiously that the Hall "could be used for a hundred things but music wasn't one of them." It had also been said of it that it was the only concert hall in the world where there could be heard two concerts for the price of one! Douglas sought the advice of the Building Research Station and the resultant somewhat elaborate scheme did the trick—at least for the time being. It entailed the provision of a 40 feet wide screen hung by cables from the roof over the platform and operated by winches; a number of 20 feet high wooden screens and accompanying drapes placed round the orchestra; and a sound reflector placed on the floor between the audience and conductor. To enable the reflector to be placed in position some rows of seats had to be removed.

The concerts commenced at 6.30 p.m. so that they could finish early in view of the black-out. The great dome was blacked-out by means of a canvas screen and notices were placed in different parts of the Hall giving information about the situation of air raid shelters and instructions on what to do should a raid be imminent.

The main concert of the first season was in honour of the centenary of the birth of Dvořák and included the playing of the Czech national anthem, not just part of the homage to the great composer, but also in token of remembrance of the Nazi occupation of his homeland. There was also an Anglo-American concert which artistically could be said to have been prophetically the forerunner of the military alliance so soon to be forged by the two nations.

After two years under the promotion of the Royal Philharmonic Society the Proms reverted to the control of the B.B.C. on 11th February 1942. Had the Corporation not made this decision when it did it is almost certain that it would have lost them as Harold Holt Limited had aleady made a firm offer to sponsor and manage them. That season the concerts were shared by the B.B.C. Symphony Orchestra and the L.P.O. under three conductors—Wood, Cameron and Sir Adrian Boult. The season was distinguished by the first performances in Britain of Shostakovich's 7th Sympony (*Leningrad*), composed within the city during its long and devastating but heroic siege, and Britten's *Sinfonia da Requiem*. The same orchestras and conductors were engaged in 1943, but due to illness Sir Henry only appeared at the beginning and end of the season. That these concerts were successful in spite of the exigencies of the times is illustrated by ticket sales in 1941 amounting to £17,000; the following year they increased to £26,000; and in 1943 sales totalled £36,000. On average attendances were about half the Hall's capacity.

The following year the Proms Golden Jubilee coincided with Hitler's penultimate air attack on London and the South East of England. The V1 or "Doodlebug" was not a weapon with which to trifle and it was decided that the season should be curtailed in the interests of safety. The incident which prompted this decision came at the end of June during a performance of Arnold Bax's Violin Concerto in E Minor by Eda Kersey. The motors of a V1 cut out as it passed over the Hall and although the music continued as if nothing of consequence had happened the resulting explosion was too near for comfort. The next day the B.B.C. attended a meeting at the Ministry of Home Security and it was decided reluctantly to close the Hall, but it was re-opened less than three months later. The year was the first to feature three orchestras, the L.S.O. joining the two which had served the previous year. Sir Henry was in charge of the opening concert on 10th June but shortly afterwards illness struck him down. The actual anniversary concert, conducted by Sir Adrian, was broadcast from Bedford, Sir Henry being too ill to conduct it himself. He died on 19th August, 50 years and nine days after he had directed the first Promenade Concert in the Queen's Hall.

Sir Henry's death resulted in Constant Lambert taking his place in the two post-War seasons, with the L.S.O. replacing the L.P.O. In 1947 Lambert in turn was replaced by Sir Malcolm Sargent, and Stanford Robinson joined the conducting team as associate.

If any single name comes to mind as synonymous with post-war Prom seasons it would be that of Malcolm Sargent. For nearly 20 years he graced the conductor's rostrum with the ebullience and elan of a much younger man, characteristics which did much to endear him to the Promenaders with whom he achieved an affinity which probably no one else is ever likely to do. His bubbling enthusiasm and charismatic charm stayed with him through advancing years and the disease that was slowly consuming him until he made his farewell appearance at the last night of the 1967 season on 16th September. Colin Davis had conducted the concert and at the end Sir Malcolm slowly walked onto the platform, said a few words and departed for the last time from the scene of so many of his triumphs; the last of which had been the final concert of the previous year, played on 17th September, the first of that season having been his 500th appearance.

Three weeks after his moving farewell he died, mourned by thousands of his faithful followers. His beloved Promenaders decided to establish a memorial to his memory and this resulted in the foundation of the Malcolm Sargent Fund for cancer relief for children, a most worthy cause which would without any doubt have received his commendation and blessing. In January each year there is a concert to raise money for the charity.

During Sir Malcolm's reign he had been joined at varying times as associates by Trevor Harvey, John Hollingsworth and Maurice Miles and in the 1950s

Sir Malcolm Sargent's last Prom, the final concert of the 1966 season. *Royal Albert Hall*

new ground was broken with invitations to guest orchestras and conductors. In this way the Hallé Orchestra made its first appearance under Sir John Barbirolli; as did the Royal Philharmonic Orchestra (R.P.O.) under its founder, Beecham; the Bournemouth Symphony Orchestra under Charles Groves; the National Youth Orchestra under Boult; and the B.B.C. Concert Orchestra. The middle year of this decade will also be remembered because of an unusual occurrence at the last night when the Greek pianist, Gina Bachauer, played John Ireland's Concerto. Before the concert she had received a communication from an anonymous writer threatening to shoot her if she played that night. Detectives mingled with the audience but happily nothing untoward occurred, though it must have been an unsettling experience for the soloist. Two years after this peculiar incident the centenary of Elgar's birth was marked by the first Prom performance of *The Dream of Gerontius*; and the 50th anniversary of Grieg's death was acknowledged by the reappearance from retirement of his famous compatriot, Kirsten Flagstad, making her Prom debut, an event surely much too long delayed. Another Norwegian, Robert Riefling, played the Piano Concerto.

Changes in programme selection were now very much in the air. In 1958 in commemoration of the centenary of Puccini's birth, Act 3 of *Tosca* was performed, the first time a complete act of any opera had been presented. Now it is commonplace for complete operas to be given in addition to large scale choral works and medieval, baroque, chamber and even electronic avant-garde music. A lot of these changes were brought about by Sir William Glock who was appointed B.B.C. Music Controller in 1959 and as such had the responsibility of programme planning. The choice of music was placed on a much broader base; for instance in 1961 the highlight was undoubtedly the first appearance of the full Glyndebourne Company with Geraint Evans and Richard Lewis performing Mozart's *Don Giovanni*. Three years later chamber music was introduced and television made frequent appearances by transmitting ten concerts to an estimated audience of 50,000,000, although the first night had been shown as far back as 1953 and the last night the year afterwards. The season also marked the retirement at the age of 80 of Cameron after 24 years as a Prom conductor. His retirement coincided with an increase in the number of guest conductors and with orchestras as well. Foreign conductors appeared with a flourish for the first time in 1963; truly a star-studded cosmopolitan company—Sir Georg Solti from Hungary; Silvio Varviso from Switzerland; Leopold Stokowski from the United States (though in fact he was born in London and died at his home in Hampshire); and Carlo Maria Guilini and Luigi Nono from Italy. Three years later the first overseas orchestra made its appearance; the Moscow Radio Orchestra played four concerts under the direction of its principal conductor, Gennadi Rozhdestvensky, a prophetic coincidence since in later years he held the same position with the B.B.C. Symphony Orchestra. The Russian visitors also broke new ground when they performed at the first planned Sunday concert; planned because there had been a prior Sunday Prom of 11th July 1943. This had occurred because the Ministry of Information had taken over the Hall at short notice on the previous Wednesday when the concert should have been performed, "for a meeting in honour of China on the occasion of the sixth anniversary of the outbreak of the Sino-Japanese War." Sunday concerts are now a regular feature of each season.

1966 was the year Sir Arthur Bliss and Havergal Brian celebrated respectively their 75th and 90th birthdays and both were suitably acknowledged by performances of the composers' works.

In 1968 there was another break with tradition when the opening night was a Friday instead of the customary Saturday; it was the occasion of a concert of all British works in memory of Sir Malcolm—Vaughan Williams' *Serenade to Music*; Walton's Viola Concerto with Peter Schidlof the soloist; and Elgar's Symphony No. 2 in E Flat played by the B.B.C. Symphony Orchestra conducted by Davis. The recently completed bronze bust of Sir Malcolm by William Timyn was on display in the Hall, which now has a permanent reminder of Sir Malcolm in John Gilroy's painting which hangs in the Foyer and was presented by the immediate past President of the Council, the late Sir Louis Gluckstein. The U.S.S.R. Symphony Orchestra conducted by Evgeny Svetlanov gave four concerts that season with David Oistrakh joining them for violin concerto performances. Two major works received particular acclaim—Bach's *St Matthew*

Passion and *The Trojans* by Berlioz; the latter was performed on a Sunday, commencing at 4.30 p.m. with an hour's intermission for supper at 6 p.m. So 1966 and 1968 broke new ground and indeed so did the intervening year with a costumed production of Britten's *The Burning Fiery Furnace.* This production by the English Opera Group was performed on a 24 feet square platform erected in the centre of the Arena which has been used since for chamber and other small scale works. The 1967 season also introduced Prom audiences for the first time to the Concertgebouw and Polish Radio Orchestras, conducted respectively by Bernard Haitink and Jan Krenz; and Mstislav Rostropovich played Dvořák's Cello Concerto, an event marred by the presence outside the Hall of banner carrying demonstrators. An incident all the more regrettable because a few years later this great Russian virtuoso took up residence in the West having found conditions intolerable in his homeland.

The opening concert of the 1969 season was a performance of Berlioz *Requiem* with Davis conducting the B.B.C. Symphony Orchestra and soloist, Ronald Dowd. This work requires enormous forces and four brass bands were spread round the Gallery. Four days afterwards, on 21st July, the 150th anniversary of the Prince Consort's birth was celebrated in the presence of the Duke of Edinburgh by performances of Handel's *Water Music* and Mendelssohn's *Hymn of Praise*; the New Philharmonia Orchestra and Chorus were conducted by Rudolf Schwarz with Vivien Townley, Janet Coster and John Mitchinson in the solo roles. That same season, for the first time, dancing was introduced—to Stravinsky's *Renard*; there was also Luciano Berio's "pop" composition, *Sinfonia*, written for the Swingle Singers and orchestra; Wilfrid Meller's *Yeibichai* for orchestra, jazz trio, chorus, soprano and scat singer; and three appearances by the Czech Philharmonic Orchestra under Vaclav Neuman.

The 1970 season was the 75th anniversary of the founding of the Proms and also the bicentenary of Beethoven's birth, celebrated in style with the *Choral Fantasia*, the *Missa Solemnis*, and a monumental performance of the *Diabelli Variations* by Alfred Brendel; two rarely heard works were performed also—the *Cantata on the Death of Emperor Joseph II* and the original version of *Fidelio*, known as *Leonora.* Completely new and daring ground in programme planning was broken on 13th August when three orchestras, each with its own conductor, played a complete concert of avant-garde music beginning at 10 p.m. One orchestra comprised 60 strings; another 34 wind instruments; and the third was made up of keyboard, percussion and harps. The purpose of this extraordinary arrangement was to perform a work called *Triple Music II* by Tim Souster, although there was another attraction in the appearance of the Soft Machine, a "pop" group which, according to Henry Pleasants of the *International Herald Tribune*, had "a bigger following among European intellectuals than with British pop fans . . . and banged, pounded, doodled and tooted for three quarters of an hour without a break and, goodness knows, without a song.

According to advance notice their offerings included '*Esthers Nose Job*' and '*Out-Bloody-Rageous.*' *Could be!*" Another sufferer described the performance as "a 40 minute offering of seemingly aimless doodlings." However, to square matters with Beethoven and erase the unpleasant memories harboured by Mr Pleasants, it must be placed on record that the great Mr Handel's *Messiah* was performed for the first time at a Prom. That same season, on 28th August, Barbirolli should have conducted a programme of works by Beethoven, Delius, Sibelius and Vaughan Williams but it became his memorial concert conducted by Groves, Sir John having died earlier in the year.

The next break with tradition was in 1971 when the Hall was forsaken on three occasions for performances staged at the Royal Opera House, Westminster Cathedral and the Round House. Also Indian music was introduced for the first time when Raga was presented by the famous sitar-player, Imrat Khan.

A year later Sir William Walton celebrated his 70th birthday and by way of greeting a special concert was given by the L.S.O. under André Previn at which Act II of *Troilus and Cressida* was presented. Also that season the first orchestra from the Orient made its debut—the N.H.K. Symphony Orchestra of Japan conducted by Hiroyuki Iwaki playing two contemporary native works in its programme. The Proms for many years have featured premieres of works specially commissioned by the B.B.,C. and 1973 was no exception except that three of the four composers were women—Nicola Le Fanu *(The Hidden Landscape)*, Thea Musgrave (a Viola Concerto played by her husband, Peter Mark), and Priaulx Rainier *(Plöermel)*. The odd man was out Lennox Berkeley (Sinfonia Concertante for oboe and chamber orchestra).

By the time Glock retired at the end of 1972 the Prom scene had changed dramatically from when he had taken over responsibility and now nearly a decade later his format still essentially prevails under his successor, Robert Ponsonby.

Great orchestras and conductors bring in their train great solo performers although many were comparatively unknown when they made their debut. One

Queuing for the last night of the Proms. *Royal Albert Hall*

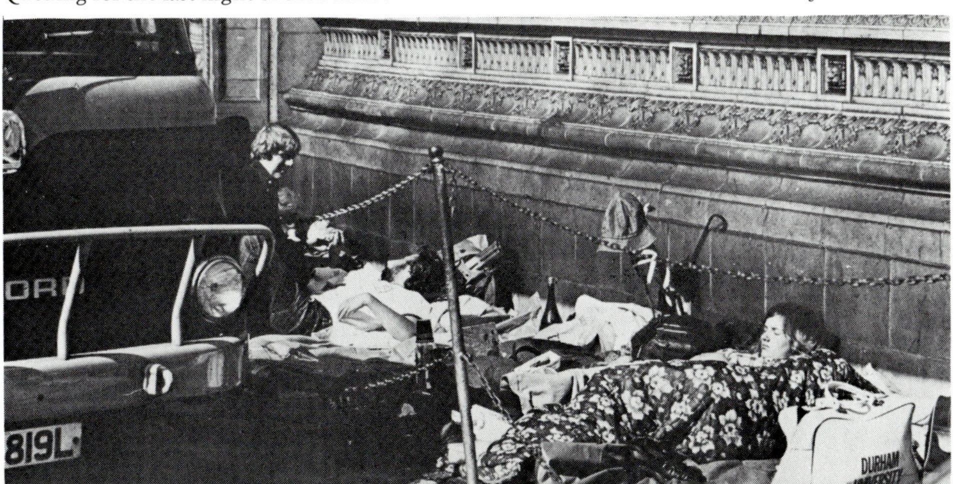

unknown made a sensational name for himself on 7th August 1974 when the L.S.O. conducted by Previn was in the middle of a performance of Carl Orff's *Carmina Burana.* The baritone soloist, Thomas Allen, was overcome by the heat, collapsed and had to be carried off the platform; his understudy, Dr Christopher Hood, was in the chorus and went off stage to attend to Allen. Urged on by his friends in the audience, Patrick McCarthy went backstage and spoke to officials, explaining that he was a professional singer with the Arts Council's Opera for All Company, that he was conversant with the score and willing to take Allen's place. Whatever qualms the officials may have had they quickly suppressed, as indeed they more or less had to do, and agreed to let McCarthy try his luck. Meanwhile the performance was continuing and no doubt all on stage and in the audience got quite a surprise when the unknown figure walked on and took his place next to the other soloists. Happily McCarthy let down neither himself, the other performers nor the audience and had the satisfaction of seeing his exploit seized upon by the national press and the following Sunday being able to watch the drama on television since the cameras had recorded the performance for later showing.

1974 also broke new ground with the introduction of brass bands playing works by Elgar, Grainger, Holst and Harrison Birtwistle; the Black Dyke Mills and Grimethorpe Colliery Bands from Yorkshire were conducted by Elgar Howarth.

The very next year there was another unusual occurrence when on 14th August London was hit by violent thunderstorms with torrential rain and hail which disrupted traffic on the roads, railways and Underground; to such an extent that the B.B.C. Symphony Orchestra's co-principal flautist, Christine Messiter, was late in arriving at the Hall and the concert was delayed.

1977 was the year of the Queen's Silver Jubilee and the opening night was graced by the presence of the Duke and Duchess of Kent who listened to a programme of all British music, a theme which also monopolised the second and third night's programmes.

What makes the Promenade Concerts the unique musical events that they are and causes wonder and astonishment to so many visiting foreign artistes when they make their debut in the great Hall before an audience of several thousands? Perhaps it is the sheer size of the building and audience; perhaps the wide range of music performed each season by so many fine orchestras, conductors, soloists and choirs from all over the world; and also perhaps the infectious and rapturous enthusiasm of the Promenaders packed like sardines on the Arena floor in the heat of mid-Summer; cooled perhaps by considering the goldfish swimming in the fountain, traditionally placed each season in their midst, or by the benign gaze of Sir Henry Wood's bronze bust, also traditionally placed each season on a plinth just below the organ console where it receives on each first night a laurel wreath from two privileged Promenaders. It is a

The last night of the 1978 Promenade season, with Sir Charles Groves conducting. *Lauri Tjurin*

reminder not only of the founder but also of Queen's Hall, because it was rescued intact from the smoking ruins after the bombing. It is the work of Donald Gilbert and was unveiled by Sir Walford Davies at Sir Henry's Golden Jubilee concert in 1938, referred to again in the next chapter. After the bombing the bust was found a home at the Royal Academy of Music from whence it is moved each year to the Hall for the Prom season.

The fountain is of about five feet diameter and, as well as goldfish, contains ornamental rocks and is bedecked with flowers. Apart from its aesthetic appearance it helps to maintain humidity on hot Summer evenings and breaks up the tightly packed humanity crammed into the Arena, thereby serving the practical purpose of a form of crush barrier.

So great is the demand to be present at the first and last night rituals that applications for tickets always exceed supply and so are subject to the luck—or otherwise—of a ballot; those with the luck are allocated seats, that is all except the Promenaders who are only guaranteed admission and therefore have to queue in hope of obtaining the best standing vantage point—a case of first come best served. 1947 was the first year that the balloting system operated and annually there are now about 28,000 applications for some 5,200 seats. In addition there is standing room for approximately 1,250 in the Arena and a hundred less in the Gallery.

The last night has become a ritualistic occasion of mascots, balloons, paper darts, streamers and flags complementing *Rule Britannia*, *Jerusalem*, the *Fantasia on British Sea-songs* and *Land of Hope and Glory* and finally, before the National Anthem, the conductor saying a few words of praise and flattery to the Promenaders and reminding them all to meet again the following year. The penultimate last nights have also developed into something of a set piece occasion with performances of Beethoven's Choral Symphony, first played on the last Friday in 1945 and followed ever since.

Satisfactory listening in the cavernous vastness of the Hall would be impossible without some mechanical assistance and to this end there are twin banks of amplifiers to aid the performers to project their instrumentation and voices to the live audiences. Apart from the first two years of the Second World War the Proms have been promoted by the B.B.C. which took over their operation as long ago as 1927, when the first transmissions were made. These have gone on ever since and are relayed nightly on either Radios 3 or 4; the World Service also transmits many of the concerts and some are televised live or video taped for later showing. By one means or another it has been estimated that 100,000,000 listeners and viewers are reached in addition to those sitting—or standing—in the Hall.

The even tenor, however, was shattered in June 1980 when the Musicians' Union called out its members on strike in protest against the B.B.C.'s decision to axe five of its orchestras for economic reasons. One was the Scottish Symphony Orchestra which has played at the Proms for a number of years. Its proposed demise drew protests from a number of eminent musicians, questions were asked in Parliament and in the end two of the five orchestras, including the Scottish, were reprieved; members of the other three achieved fairly reasonable free-lance terms after their units ceased to exist in March, 1981. Before the dispute was settled the Proms had been affected rather seriously and the season did not commence until 7th August, nearly three weeks late. It was during these troubled times that the Musicians' Union was refused the use of the Hall in June for the purpose of staging two concerts in aid of its Hardship Fund. The reason for the Council's refusal was that it was considered inappropriate to let the Hall to an organisation bent on condemning the actions of one of its best clients—too much a case of "biting the hand that fed" it was felt.

CHAPTER SIX

The Sound of Music

FROM THE start it was always contemplated, not least by Henry Cole, that the Royal Albert Hall should be the scene of great musical performances and one of the principal concert halls in the land. Certainly so far as the arts aspect of the "arts and sciences" connotation is concerned music is far and away the leader and there is little doubt that it is the subject that first comes to mind when mention is made of the Hall. Albert would be delighted if he was alive today and able to look back on a century of music making by most of the world's greatest exponents.

It is nearly 40 years since the Proms were by force of circumstances moved to the Hall but during the previous 70 years it had witnessed some of the great moments of musical history and the period after the Second World War has continued the tradition. Mention has been made already of some of the earliest performances but there were many more of interest and merit before the turn of the century, not least the arrival in May, 1877 of the 240 strong Bayreuth Festival Orchestra with choir and soloists to stage a festival of Wagner's works conducted by the composer and Hans Richter; at the series of eight concerts all the Master's works were represented except *Parsifal* which had to wait another seven years before the Royal Albert Hall Choral Society gave the first concert performance. The appearance in England of the Company was remarkable in that it occurred only a year after the inauguration of this now famous festival in the newly erected Festival Theatre. The leader of the Orchestra was the famous virtuoso, August Wilhelmj, who died in London in 1908 having been for the last 14 years of his life principal violin professor at the Guildhall School of Music. Wagner's ability as a conductor was strictly limited and fortunately he recognised this so that he only directed the occasional piece, leaving the bulk of the work to Richter. When Richter was in charge Wagner used to sit in an armchair facing the audience.

Two years before Wagner appeared on the scene Verdi had conducted those memorable performances of his *Requiem* and now three years after Wagner came Charles Camille Saint-Saëns to give a series of organ recitals in May 1880. A talented pianist, composer of considerable repute and organist of the Madelaine in Paris for some 20 years, he was a frequent visitor to London and even before giving the recitals he had an indirect link with the Hall in that he had studied privately under Gounod, the man who had caused so much trouble for the Council a few years previously.

Verdi from Italy, Wagner from Germany, Saint-Saëns from France and then Antonin Dvořák from what is now Czechoslovakia but was then Bohemia. His first visit to England was in 1884 to conduct his *Stabat Mater* and other compositions and he enthusiastically recorded the pleasure it had given him. "On Monday March 10th there was the first rehearsal with the choir in the Albert Hall, an enormous building in which there is easily room for as many as 12,000 people. When I appeared on the platform I was welcomed with thunderous and lasting applause; a long time passed before there was a moment of quiet again. I was so profoundly impressed by such a cordial ovation that I could not speak even a word. On the next day there was a rehearsal with the orchestra and in the evening with the soloists. But I must indicate shortly what is the size of the choir and orchestra. Please do not be afraid! There are 250 sopranos, 160 altos, 180 tenors and 250 basses. The orchestra, 16 violins, 16 cellos, 16 double basses. The impression of such a mighty body was indeed enchanting. It is quite indescribable. It all went off as well as I could possibly have wished. From all I have gained the conviction that a new, and with God's will, a happier period is growing for me here in England . . . The English are a good, cordial, and music loving nation. It is well known that if they are fond of anyone they remain loyal to him. May God grant that this may happen in my case too!"

The great man was of course way out with his estimate of the Hall's capacity but after such graceful and wholehearted compliments he could be forgiven for the exaggeration.

To have composers of such calibre appearing at the infant Hall in the space of only nine years was something of which the Council could well be proud but yet another great occasion was to fall within that same time span. In June 1882 Adelina Patti, the most celebrated soprano of the last 40 years of Victoria's reign, sang in the Hall for the first time although by then she had graced the stage of the Royal Opera House for 20 years with the Royal Italian Opera. It was the "Queen of Song" who popularised *Home Sweet Home* from an obscure opera called *Clari* by Henry Bishop, who also has another claim to fame in that he was knighted by the Queen in 1842, the first musician ever to be so honoured. His famous song owes little to the opera and almost everything to Patti, who probably sang it every time she appeared on a concert platform. Four years after her debut Patti gave the first of a series of recitals which were to span very nearly the next 30 years; each year three or four were presented and they could be guaranteed a sell-out, such was her fame and popularity. Her formal farewell appearance was on 1st December 1906, amongst the "supporting cast" being Ferruccio Busoni and Pablo Sarasate; that these two should be "also rans" to the great singer is surprising perhaps but at least it emphasises her magnetism, as was the case just over a year before when on 10th November 1905 her "supporters" included Kirkby Lunn, Fritz Kreisler and Mark Hambourg.

Similarly the greatest British baritone of the day, Charles Santley, often used to appear on the same platform as Patti but always with secondary billing. In all Patti gave 64 recitals at the Hall and in spite of her 1906 "farewell" her very last appearance was not until 20th October 1914.

The 7th December 1892 was another significant day in the Hall's musical history because it was then that Clara Butt made her professional debut in Sir Arthur Sullivan's religious cantata *The Golden Legend*. Her specialities were the National Anthem, *Abide With Me* and *Land of Hope and Glory* and these she sang with gusto, frequently accompanied by the great organ. The latter piece had been used by Sir Edward Elgar as the refrain in his *Pomp and Circumstance March No. 1* composed in the first years of this century and ideally suited to the mood of the times.

The years of the First World War were ideally suited to Clara Butt's effectiveness as an arouser of national pride and fervour and this was amply manifested on 13th May 1915 when the King and Queen and Princess Mary attended a concert in aid of the British Red Cross Society. Clara Butt paid all the concert expenses and then did her best to dispose of the seats at the highest going-rate. Boxes sold for £200 and single seats were snapped up for £20, very large sums for that time; D. A. Thomas, who later became Lord Rhondda, had just survived the sinking of the *Lusitania* and was asked by Clara Butt, probably as a thank offering, to subscribe £1,000 for the Prince of Wales' box, the seats to be allocated to wounded soldiers. Thomas apparently was willing and happy to comply with the request. The concert opened with the massed bands of the Brigade of Guards playing the National Anthem of which Clara sang the second verse; when that was over there was a great waving of flags by the audience, each person on entering the Hall having been given a white silk flag for the purpose; a rather curious choice considering its connotation and when the obvious emblem would seem to have been the Union Jack. The programme was designed for such an occasion and was entirely predictable; Kennerley Rumford had come straight from France, where he was a Red Cross driver, and appeared in khaki to join Clara in what was no more than a popular programme but one that fitted the occasion. There was Sir Edward German's *Coronation March* and *The Yeomen of England*; *A Ballad of the Ranks*; *Hymn for Aviators* by Sir Hubert Parry; *The Home Flag*; Stanford's *The King's Highway*; *The Lost Chord* by Sullivan and, of course, *Abide with Me*, specially requested by the Queen in a message written in her own hand to Clara. There was also the *1812 Overture* which the conductor of the bands, Capt. J. MacKenzie Rogan, is credited with introducing to British audiences. Finally and inevitably came *Land of Hope and Glory* in which Clara was joined by the bands, organ and audience.

Another concert at which Clara gave her services was for wounded soldiers, many of whom were brought to the Hall on stretchers. Then just over a year after hostilities ceased one of her Subscription Concerts was in aid of St Dunstan's after care of blinded soldiers and sailors. It was given on 9th December 1919 in the presence of the King and Queen and apart from Clara those taking part were Kennerley Rumford, Bronislaw Hubermann and Lady Tree. Carrie Tubb sang the National Anthem, and Emma Albani and other leading members of the profession volunteered to form a choir.

Another well loved performer of the period was the great Irish tenor, John McCormack, and two of the songs he made world famous received their première in the Hall. On 14th March 1908 *I Hear You Calling Me* and in April 1932 *Bless This House.* The former had been composed by his accompanist, Charles Marshall, who had despaired of ever getting anyone to publish it but McCormack's performance not only put it on the market but also sent it round the world.

George Szell made his first appearance in England on 15th November 1908 at the ripe old age of eleven years when he played Mendelssohn's *Capriccio in B Minor* with the L.S.O. conducted by Landon Ronald; not content with one performance he played again a fortnight later. Child prodigies are not uncommon but many are here today and gone tomorrow, burned out by their precocity, but this was not young Szell's fate; he went on to achieve fame, not as an instrumentalist but as conductor of the Cleveland Orchestra. Few present at these concerts could have contemplated what the future had in store for him but they were certainly in at the beginning of a long and distinguished career.

Ten days after Szell first burst on to the London scene another youngster of promise appeared on the same platform in the person of Mischa Elman, aged 17, giving one of his earliest recitals. He was destined to achieve as great a fame as Szell but as a violin virtuoso. On this occasion he played the Brahms concerto and one of Paganini's with the L.S.O. under Emil Mlynarski. Young though Szell and Elman were, they were far older than Willy Ferrero when he strode onto the stage on 6th May 1914; he was just seven and a half years old when he mounted the rostrum to conduct the 90 players of the New Symphony Orchestra in the Overture, *William Tell*, *Serenade Maueresque*, by Elgar, the Overture *Egmont* and selections from *Parsifal*, *A Midsummer Night's Dream* and *The Damnation of Faust*; a catholicity of taste that well might have daunted a mature exponent of the conductor's art for one evening's work. The young man had appeared already before the Czar and Czarina and was hailed with some justification as the youngest orchestral conductor in the world, a record which he probably still holds. Appropriately the proceeds of young Willy's efforts went to the Hospital for Sick Children, Great Ormond Street, London. This mini genius did not play an instrument, did not read music, conducted from memory and was mad on toy motor cars! After listening to Willy's first rehearsal with the Orchestra Landon Ronald wrote in the *Daily Mail*, "I think he is the most unaccountable genius I have ever come across. To me it is the greatest mystery, because he seems to know at his age more than men who have spent their lives studying conducting. I am up against something that I cannot account for at all. It would be easier for me to understand if the boy knew the elements of music. As it is he is simply a born conductor. I am judging him on the most critical basis." *The Times*, *Sunday Times*, *Telegraph*, *Standard*, *Yorkshire Post* and *Referee* all featured news items about Willy's performance.

It would seem nobody appeared to rival the young maestro for another 33 years and then in January, 1947, 14-year-old Pierino Gamba directed the Philharmonia Orchestra in a Beethoven programme consisting of the Overture *Egmont*, and the 1st and 5th Symphonies. Just under three years later on 11th December 1949, 10-year-old Roberto Benzi conducted the L.S.O. in a programme that included *In the Steppes of Central Asia*, the suite from *The Nutcracker*, *The Dance of the Hours*, Mozart's 40th Symphony, and the *Capriccio Espagnol.* Of this young trio only Gamba went on to make an international career for himself, Ferrero and Benzi disappearing from the scene apparently as suddenly as they had appeared upon it.

Yehudi Menuhin, who gave his first recital in the Hall at the age of 13. *Lauri Tjurin*

No mention of young people making their mark in the Hall can leave out Yehudi Menuhin who gave his first recital in the Hall at the age of 13 years on 10th November 1929. Two years later he appeared again and with the L.P.O. conducted by Beecham played two concertos—Bach's No. 2 in E Major and Mozart's No. 7 in D Major K271a. The event that really brought him to the notice of the musical world came in 1932 when he tackled the formidable task of performing Elgar's Concerto in B Minor with the composer conducting; this of course became a legendary performance and set him on an international career which happily he is still pursuing for the pleasure of all who love great music and great playing.

In June 1908 there was a recital by Serge Koussevitzky who was a virtuoso of the double-bass and, one imagines, his appearance was really one of those occasions strictly for the connoisseur. Later he was to achieve even greater fame as conductor of the Boston Symphony Orchestra from 1924-49. In March of the following year Elena Gerhardt gave a recital accompanied by Artur Nikisch who had become famous as conductor of the Berlin Philharmonic and Leipzig Gewandhaus Orchestras. In September the same year Enrico Caruso gave a recital and in the summer of 1910 Melba made yet another appearance at the Hall.

On 29th May 1911 the Royal Amateur Orchestral Society and the Royal Choral Society conducted by Sir Frank Bridge were joined by several well known soloists, including Clara Butt, Kirkby Lunn, Agnes Nicholls, Ben Davies,

Leonard Bernstein, conductor of the New York Philharmonic Orchestra, taking part in an international celebrity concert on 3rd June 1976. *Royal Albert Hall*

Edmund Burke and Watkin Mills in a programme of popular works performed in the presence of the King and Queen. Four days later Nikisch conducted the L.S.O. with Wilhelm Backhaus as soloist and a fortnight after that Louisa Tetrazzini sang the *Mad Scene* from *Hamlet* and then, as if to show her versatility, Martini's *Plaisir D'Amour.*

Melba and Jan Kubelik gave a joint recital on 4th May 1913 and they were followed a fortnight afterwards by Backhaus, Kreisler and Maggie Teyte. The latter had made her name at the Paris Opera and it was from there that another prima donna, Mlle. Verlet, came a month later to star with Vladimir Rozing, a tenor from the St Petersburg Opera, and Elman. Then came Jacques Thibaud for a recital on 9th November; he should have appeared in October of the following year but on the first of the month his agent sent a telegram from Paris to the promoter in London stating that Thibaud had been refused permission to leave France by the authorities. It is possible the war had something to do with the prohibition but, whatever the reason, Thibaud did not arrive and W. H. Squire took his place.

On 8th January 1913 Maggie Teyte and Joseph Szigeti gave a joint recital and on 27th February there was a performance of *The Dream of Gerontius* with Clara Butt, Gervaise Elwes and Robert Radford. Later in the year on 27th November the Royal Choral Society presented a double bill of Saint-Saens *The Promised Land*, to a text by Herman Kleen, and Coleridge-Taylor's *A Tale of Old Japan*, a setting of a poem by Alfred Noyes.

The months of 1914 leading up to the outbreak of the First World War saw no decline in the quality of concerts and recitals or in the celebrities participating in them. In May, Maggie Teyte, Kreisler and Backhaus appeared on the Sunday platform, followed a week later by Kubelik; in early June came Tetrazzini and on the 24th of the month Vladimir Pachmann to give his last recital, although in fact this was a false farewell since he reappeared from retirement in September, 1918.

The first really memorable concert after the war was when the Royal Choral Society celebrated its Diamond Jubilee five months prematurely on 7th May 1921 in the presence of the King and Queen, Princess Mary and three members of the Royal Family who had been present at the Hall's opening ceremony 50 years before—the Duke of Connaught (President of the Royal Choral Society) and Princesses Christian and Beatrice. Also in the audience were Lady Patricia Ramsay and the President of the Royal Albert Hall Corporation, Earl Howe. A few words are necessary here about the brainchild of a clarinetist, Charles Draper, who had founded the New Symphony Orchestra early in the century and saw it incorporated as a limited liability company in 1907. The previous year Beecham began an association with it and introduced it into the private salons of London society, it being small in size but with a refined style. Appearances were made in large towns under Beecham, Ronald and Coates and in 1920 the name was changed to The Royal Albert Hall Orchestra. Now on this Jubilee occasion it was conducted by Landon Ronald and the Royal Choral Society Orchestra and Choir were under Sir Frederick Bridge, a total of 1,000 performers all told. The Choir was placed half on one side of the organ and half on the other, the altos on the left wearing blue sashes and the sopranos on the right red sashes. At the time the Choir was made up of 250 sopranos, 170 altos, 170 tenors and 250 basses. The organ was played by H. L. Balfour and the piano by Arnold Greir and the soloists were Carrie Tubb, Kirkby Lunn, Davies and Radford. Elgar, Stanford and Alexander C. Mackenzie conducted their own works. The programme included *Onaway! Awake, Beloved* (Davies); *The Jewel Song* (Tubb); *Land of Hope and Glory* (Lunn); two of the *Songs of the Sea* (Radford); and the Overture, *Britannia*. The profit of £104. 9s. 4d. (£104.47) was divided equally between the participating bodies, the soloists each received five guineas (£5.25) and Balfour received two guineas (£2.10) for "incidental expenses." In the course of events seven of the original male members who had joined during the first season in 1871 were presented to the King.

The Society had been founded in October that year as the Royal Albert Hall Choral Society and performed under that name until 1888 when, at the command of Queen Victoria, it was renamed The Royal Choral Society (R.C.S.). Long before receiving this Royal approbation of quality and worth its administration had passed to a Committee separate from that administering the Hall; this was in 1876 but in spite of official severance of its affairs from the Council and Corporation it has maintained very close ties with the Hall right down to the present time. Its first conductor was the redoubtable Charles Gounod who was successively succeeded by Sir Joseph Barnby, Sir Frederick Bridge and H. L. Balfour. Bridge received his early training at Rochester Cathedral and was later organist at Manchester Cathedral and Westminster Abbey—from which appointment came his nickname of "Westminster Bridge". He maintained and supported the Choir through the difficulties engendered by the First World War and by the time he retired in 1922 he had celebrated his Silver Jubilee with the Choir; he it was who instigated in 1912 the popular Carol Concerts which still are a principal feature of the Choir's annual programme. When Balfour took over he was assisted by a series of Guest Conductors, among whom were Sir Hugh Allen, Eugene Goosens, Sir Landon Ronald and Albert Coates; then in 1928 Malcolm Sargent was appointed permanent conductor, a post he retained until his much lamented death in 1967.

During the Second World War the Choir moved its base to the Queen's Hall when the Royal Albert Hall was closed at the commencement of hostilities. Here under Sargent's direction it performed with the L.P.O. the last ever concert on 10th May 1941. Appropriately perhaps the work was *The Dream of Gerontius* by arguably perhaps the most English of English composers, Sir Edward Elgar. A few hours after the Concert the old Queen's Hall was totally destroyed in an air raid. The choir returned to the Royal Albert Hall which had been reopened and Sargent and the Choir introduced choral works to the Promenade Concerts for the first time.

On 8th January 1955 the Society gave its 1,000th performance, Sir Malcolm Sargent conducting the L.S.O. in *Messiah* with Jennifer Vyvyan, Marjorie Thomas, William Herbert and Trevor Anthony.

Since 1967 the Choir has been conducted firstly by Wyn Morris and then by Meredith Davies who is still in charge; these two and all their predecessors have each done their part in ensuring the continued admiration and affection that all lovers of great choral music must have for this group of talented amateurs who become so professional when they appear on a concert platform.

On 8th May 1972 the Society celebrated its centenary in grand style and in the presence of the Duke and Duchess of Kent. The diversity of the programme exemplified the wide range of choral music which this great body of singers performs with such devotion and mastery; after a fanfare by the Kneller Hall Trumpeters they were joined by the Orchestra in Sir Edward Elgar's setting of the National Anthem and then the concert got under way with Benjamin Britten's *Rejoice in the Lamb* and *The Music Makers* by Elgar. After the interval there was Sir William Walton's *Coronation Te Deum* written for the Coronation of Queen Elizabeth II, and Coleridge-Taylor's *Hiawatha's Wedding Feast* a reminder of the great costumed performances put on in the 1920s and 1930s. The soloists were Janet Baker, Oriel Sutherland and Richard Lewis with John Birch at the organ, and the R.P.O. was conducted by Charles Groves and Meredith Davies.

At the time the Duke of Kent was President of the Society, a position he still holds and to which he succeeded on the death of his Mother, Princess Marina, who in turn succeeded her husband upon his death in a flying accident during the Second World War after only a few months in office. Prior to 1942 there had only been two other Presidents—the Duke of Edinburgh from 1883-1900 and then the Duke of Connaught whose term spanned 42 years. Connections with the Royal Family have always been strong and each monarch in succession, starting with Queen Victoria, has been Patron of the Society.

Conductors apart the Choir has also been well supported by a succession of fine organists beginning with Sir John Stainer, the renowned instrumentalist of St Paul's Cathedral; he was followed by William Hodge, H. L. Balfour, Arnold Greir and now John Birch who is at present organist of Chichester Cathedral.

The day after the King and Queen had joined in the R.C.S. Diamond Jubilee Celebrations in 1921 they returned to the Hall for the farewell recital given by Dame Nellie Melba prior to her departure for home in Australia. In fact it was another of those "farewells" beloved of so many artistes and her final appearance did not take place for another five years. More or less in the middle of Melba's formal and actual farewells there was welcomed another great singer in 1924. On 12th October the coloratura soprano, Amalita Galli-Curci, made her debut before a capacity audience. According to the *Illustrated London News* tickets were changing hands at extraordinary prices; for instance 5/9d (29p) seats were snapped up "at a guinea and a-half" (£1.57½). Until this appearance her reputation in Britain had been established entirely by gramophone records but at the end it was clear from the prolonged and thunderous applause that London had taken her to its heart. She crowned her performance by singing *Home, Sweet Home*, accompanying herself on the piano; a nostalgic touch which must have taken back many of those present to the great days of Patti.

Apart from the R.C.S. Jubilee 1921 was notable for two other events of major importance. Firstly on 13th May there was the visit of the Choir of the Sistine Chapel in the Vatican which gave two concerts of sacred music; then on 2nd July, which was celebrated as Verdun Sunday, the famous Band of the Garde Republicaine was the attraction. In December 1924, there was a British Empire Music Festival, memorable for the playing not only of the Central Band of the R.A.F., conducted by Fl. Lieut. J. H. Amers, and the Pipers of the Scots Guards, but also of the Great Britain Women's Symphony Orchestra conducted by Gwynne Kimpton. At this time when female orchestral performers were virtually non-existent, a full symphony orchestra of them must have been little short of sensational. Unfortunately there seems to be no record of the Orchestra ever performing again at the Hall. The soloists on this occasion were Clara Butt, May Haxley, Joseph Hislop and Robert Radford with P. Mavon Ibbs at the organ and Ivor Newton at the piano.

The same year Thomas Fairbairn, who was a relative of the Fairbairn responsible for the construction of the Hall's roof and had been an engineer himself, produced a costumed version of Mascagni's opera *Cavalleria Rusticana* and scenes from Gounod's opera *Faust*. He had long since given up engineering to become a singer and later stage manager of the Moody Manners Opera Company, so was well acquainted with the intricacies and problems of musical stage productions. Criticism was mixed but Fairbairn put the adverse behind him and went ahead with arranging something far more spectacular for 1924. He confessed that for some time he had wanted to do a "spectacular" of either Mendelsohn's *Elijah* or Coleridge-Taylor's *Hiawatha*. The catalyst for the go-ahead was a request to him by the National Institute for the Blind to organise a charity production; but which had it to be? He chose the simple expedient of checking with the R.C.S. as to which of the two works had brought in the most money on the previous occasions they had been performed and *Hiawatha* just had the edge on *Elijah*. Fairbairn's 1924 production was the first of an uninterrupted, apart from 1926 due to the General Strike, annual run until 1939 when the Second World War intervened and put an end to a long running success story. One of the 1928 performances was attended by the King and Queen.

The staging of *Hiawatha* was not without its problems as the Hall lacked the back-stage facilities to be found in a theatre. Nevertheless Fairbairn was undaunted and triumphed over all the disadvantages, even utilising the stream which flows beneath the Hall for the waterfall. An enormous blue backcloth with an area of well over 1,000 square yards was hung and provided a bonus in the form of improved acoustics while half a dozen million-candle-power spot lights, complete with cooling systems to enable colour masks to be used, were placed in strategic positions; so great was the power load that prior notification of switch-on had to be given so that the electricity authorities could be prepared for the shock. At the opposite extreme there was almost complete darkness when the snow-storm was enacted, so dark that the conductor, Eugene Goosens, had a light bulb in his baton. Nowadays artistes appearing at the Hall are provided

Chief Os-Ke-Non-Ton, of the Mohawk tribe, acting the part of the Medicine Man in the Royal Choral Society's production of *Hiawatha* in 1933.

with modern toilet facilities, including showers, but in *Hiawatha* days things were much more primitive and problems were posed when it came to removing the elaborate make-up. All this was exciting and stirring stuff but perhaps the real piece-de-resistance was the appearance of a Mohawk chief, Os-Ke-Non-Ton, in one of the leading roles. He was a professional singer but most of the other participants were amateurs including the chorus, naturally provided by the R.C.S., soon to become closely associated with Sargent who also became conductor of the later *Hiawathas*. What is perhaps remarkable is that a largely amateur production should turn out so regularly to be so profitable; to the extent of contributing £700 of the Hall's total profit of £900 in 1928—and this in the space of a mere two weeks! The war ended the costumed productions of *Hiawatha* but for a few more years there were concert versions but sadly even these are no more. On 4th May 1947 the R.C.S. celebrated its 75th season with a production which featured the L.S.O. under Sargent with Arnold Greir at the organ, and Elsie Suddaby, Henry Wendon and Harold Williams.

1930 was the year of great foreign orchestras, no fewer than three world class combinations gracing the Hall's platform. Firstly, in April, came Arturo Toscanini and the Philharmonic Symphony Orchestra of New York playing in the presence of the King and Queen. They were followed on 27th and 29th of the month by the Vienna Philharmonic Orchestra under Furtwängler and on 14-16th May the Concertegebouw Orchestra of Amsterdam conducted by Willem Mengelberg. Then at the end of June there was a total change of mood with the *Daily Mail's* promotion of a Festival of English Church Music.

Two of the greatest singers of the inter-war years appeared in succeeding years—1931-2. Firstly Conchita Supervia sang songs in national costume by her compatriots—Albeniz, Granados, de Falla, Nin and Rodrigo; and then Elisabeth Schumann sang with the L.S.O. conducted by Carl Alwyn of the Vienna State Opera. 1933 was notable for another visit by the Berlin Philharmonic Orchestra (Berlin P.O.) under Fürtwangler; this was on 19th February and then on 12th November Tetrazzini gave her farewell recital.

During the Second World War concerts and recitals were still promoted but not without certain disorganisation and some trepidation. That they went on at all is a tribute not only to the performers but to their audiences as well.

After the disruption of the war events soon returned to normal and on 23rd May 1945 a concert was given under the patronage of the French Ambassador by the L.P.O. and Luton Choral Society conducted by Charles Münch with soloists Kathleen Long, Joan Cross and Gerard Souzay. During 1947 Eileen Joyce played three concertos at a single concert on 7th March—the Rachmaninov No. 2, Tchaikovsky No. 1 and the Grieg—and this could really be said to be the start of her long association with the Hall, frequently playing with the Philharmonia Orchestra and becoming well known for her habit of changing her dress during the interval of a recital.

It was not long after the end of the war before foreign orchestras, conductors and artistes were appearing once more on the platform of the Royal Albert Hall. The Vienna Philharmonic Orchestra (Vienna P.O.) came in 1947 and 1948, playing all the Beethoven symphonies on the second visit and accompanying Yehudi Menuhin in a performance of the Violin Concerto. The conductors were Bruno Walter, Furtwängler and Josef Krips. Furtwängler returned with the Orchestra in 1949 and for one of its performances the programme was of works inspired by Goethe, having been organised by the

Members of the Omsk Dance Company seen during their visit in 1967. *Royal Albert Hall*

Great Britain Goethe Festival Society to honour the 200th anniversary of his birth. Three years elapsed before the great Orchestra returned to England, this time under Clemens Krauss: and with them on 17th November Kathleen Ferrier sang Mahler's *Kindertotenlieder*. This concert proved to be the last public appearance by this greatly loved and incomparable contralto who was already stricken by cancer from which she died the following year.

The 1950s were significant for first appearances by world famous Russian soloists and ensembles—David and Igor Oistrakh, Mstislav Rostropovich and

Sviatoslav Richter, and the Leningrad Philharmonic and Moscow Radio Orchestras. Russian music has always been a popular feature of concerts and many programmes during the course of each year are given over to the works of Tchaikovsky; the Overture *1812* is always a great favourite played as it usually is with a military band, organ and cannon effects accompanying the orchestra. The "cannons" are situated in the Gallery and operated electronically from the conductor's desk.

Another work requiring enormous force is Mahler's 8th Symphony *(Symphony of a Thousand)*. When it was performed on 20th March 1959 it was the first time in the Hall for 10 years. The L.S.O. (augmented to a strength of 150), B.B.C. Chorus and Choral Society, Goldsmiths' Choral Union, Hampstead Choral Society, Emanuel School Boys' Choir and Orpington Junior Singers were conducted by Yascha Horenstein. Altogether there were 782 performers including the eight soloists—Joyce Barker, Beryl Hatt, Helen Watts, Agnes Giebel, Kerstin Meyer, Kenneth Neote, Alfred Orda and Arnold van Mill. In June, 1971 the National Philharmonic Orchestra (N.P.O.) and Chorus and the Musikverein of Düsseldorf under Rafael Frübeck de Burgos gave another performance and similar forces were assembled again on 11th December 1972 when it was performed by the Symphonica of London, New Philharmonia Chorus, Ambrosian Singers, Bruckner/Mahler Choir, London Highgate School Choir, Finchley Children's Music Group and Orpington Junior Singers under the direction of Wyn Morris. The soloists were Joyce Barker, Elizabeth Simon, Norma Burrows, Joyce Blackham, Alfreda Hodgson, Stuart Kale, Raymond Myers and Gwynne Howell. Like the "cannons" in the Gallery the upper reaches of the Hall again come in useful for the Mahler Symphony because the eight additional trombones required for the last movement are played from a box right under the roof.

Beethoven's equally rarely performed *Battle Symphony*, written to commemorate Wellington's victory over the French at Vittoria in 1813, also calls for the unusual. When it was played on 11th March 1962 by the Royal Opera House Orchestra, trumpeters and drummers from the Life Guards were employed and men of the Coldstream Guards and London Rifle Brigade exchanged fire across the Hall high up in the Boxes. Joseph Horowitz was the conductor and he said "it sounded like blue murder."

Performed even less frequently than the Mahler and Beethoven Symphonies is Havergal Brian's massive *Gothic Symphony* which only received its first performance in London in 1961 although it had been written some 40 years earlier. On 30th October 1966 it was performed in the Hall to celebrate the composer's 90th birthday and if or when it ever will be peformed again is anyone's guess. The score calls for an orchestra of 180 players, four brass groups and four large mixed choirs. The last performance was televised by the B.B.C. and broadcast on Radio 3 and the participants numbered about 700.

Fortunately popularity does not depend on immense forces and in this respect Viennese music must run neck and neck with Tchaikovsky in the public's favour, especially when the Strauss family are represented as they are on a frequent and regular basis; and what better ambassadors could Austria send than the Vienna Boys' Choir, which usually appears annually in its sailor suit uniform, although when Strauss' numbers are featured the boys very often appear in costume.

On 3rd April 1960 a recital was given by Backhaus and then from 27th June—17th July the Bolshoi Ballet was in residence with its Principal Conductor, Zhemtuzhin, directing the L.P.O. There was no scenery, just black drapes. The Soviet Ambassador in London, Aleksander Soldatov, attended a party at the Hall on the opening night.

A special event, even for the Hall, was the appearance on the platform on 28th September 1963 of three of the world's greatest violinists playing with the Moscow Philharmonic Orchestra under Kondrashin. The Oistrakhs and Yehudi Menuhin were the stars of a performance which, because it had to fit in with television scheduling, did not start until 9.15. Menuhin and David Oistrakh had been concerned the previous year in what must be a rarity even for the Albert Hall. They were due to give a performance with the R.P.O. on the evening of 23rd September but due to the concert being a sell-out it was decided to allow the public to attend the afternoon rehearsal. 4,500 took the opportunity to be present to see each soloist conduct the orchestra for the other; Oistrakh played the Beethoven Concerto and Menuhin the Brahms Concerto and they then teamed up to play Bach's Double Concerto in D Minor.

From 20th December 1963 to 19th January 1964 the London Festival Ballet with leading dancers from the Bolshoi, Kirov and other European ballet companies gave two performances daily with the L.P.O. A stage with a towering canopy over it was erected in front of the organ for the staging of the *Nutcracker*, *Swan Lake*, *Les Sylphides*, *Prince Igor*, *American Symphonette* (Morton Gould) and *Walpurgis Night* from *Faust*.

On 10th October 1964 Moiseiwitsch made his last appearance. On 27th October 1964 the N.P.O. and Chorus gave their first concert, performing Beethoven's *Choral Symphony* under Klemperer with Agnes Giebel, Marga Höffgen, Ernst Haefliger and Gustav Neidlinger, and another debut was made in 1966, that of Joan Sutherland who appeared on 20th February with the L.P.O. conducted by her husband, Richard Bonynge.

A Royal occasion with a difference happened on 25th April 1968 when the King and Queen of Denmark were present to hear a programme played by the Danish Radio Symphony Orchestra under John Pritchard. In October and November that year there were three Organ Festivals featuring Germani of the Vatican, Langlais of France, Peeters of Belgium and Schreiner of the United States as well as Kynaston and Thalben-Ball.

Leonard Bernstein conducting the London Symphony Orchestra in a Bicentennial concert on 4th July 1976. *Royal Albert Hall*

A rather unusual event of 1969 was the hiring of the Hall by 51-year-old Polish-born Dr Michael Bialoguski in order to achieve his ambition as a conductor. To do this he engaged the R.P.O. in what he thought was the only way to obtain recognition as a conductor although, in fact, he was a freelance violinist, had studied at a master conductors' course at Siena, and had also conducted the Sydney Symphony Orchestra. The enterprise cost him something in the region of £2,000. The year was also unusual because the L.P. Choir put on an unaccustomed hat when it appeared with Fairey's and Foden's Brass Bands conducted by the doyen of brass band conductors, Harry Mortimer, in "Men O'Brass and Voices."

A strange piece of eccentricity ended with the death in March 1969 of Sir Francis Cassel who had hired the Hall personally for a number of years in order to play his favourite piano compositions.

Memorial, celebratory and commemorative concerts have been regular events for very many years, one of the earliest going back to 1910 when an era came to an end with the death of Edward VII. On 22nd May a National Memorial Concert was given by the New Symphony Orchestra conducted by Sir Charles Stanford; so great was the demand for tickets that the concert had to be repeated a week later. Solemn was the occasion and solemn the music which included the Funeral Marches by Beethoven and Chopin; the *Prelude and Angel's Farewell* from *The Dream of Gerontius*; *Recompense* from Parry's *War and Peace*; Stanford's *Martyrdom*; and Sullivan's *Light World.* The soloists were Ada Crossley and Davies, and the orchestral sound was augmented by the drummers of the Grenadier Guards.

An orchestra of 472 players drawn from the Queen's Hall and London Symphony Orchestras and the Philharmonic Society were conducted by Beecham, Elgar, Ronald and Wood on 24th May 1912 when the *Titanic* Concert was given barely six weeks after the great liner had foundered in the Atlantic. It was known that the ship's band had played *Nearer my God to Thee* as the vessel sank into the icy depths off Cape Race and the concert ended with the orchestra and organ accompanying the standing audience in the singing of this beautiful hymn. The poignancy of the moment was not lost on any of those present.

Another great shipping disaster was the sinking of the *Empress of Ireland* in 1914. On 29th June there was a Memorial Concert in aid of the Lord Mayor's Fund; like the *Titanic* Concert it was given by combined orchestras—the Royal Philharmonic, Queen's Hall, London Symphony, New Symphony, Beecham Symphony, and Royal Opera House—playing under the direction of Beecham, Emile Cooper, Mylnarski, Georges Palacco, Percy Pitt, Ronald and Wood.

A memorial concert for those who had died in the war was held in 1916 in the presence of the King and Queen and Ambassadors and Ministers of the Allies. They heard a performance of Verdi's *Requiem* and in addition the R.C.S. sang *With Proud Thanksgiving*, with Elgar conducting, in memory of its own members who had died on active service.

The Memorial Concert for George V took place on 4th February 1936 with the L.P.O. conducted by Ronald, Sargent and Wood, and the 180 strong band and 50 trumpeters of the Royal Military School of Music conducted by Major Adlus. Percy Kahn was at the piano, the organist was Herbert Dawson and the soloists were Eva Turner who sang *The Lord is my Light* and *Let the Bright Seraphim*; Astra Desmond whose contributions were *Dido's Lament* and *The Angel's Farewell*; and John McCormack who rendered *Caro Amor* and *Where ere You Walk*. There was a women's choir dressed in white with black rosettes to sing Harwood's *Requiem Aeturnum*, Purcell's *Evening Hymn*; and *Jerusalem.* The trumpeters played fanfares by Davies, Bliss and Bax and the band and orchestra played the Beethoven and Chopin Funeral Marches; *Venus* from *The Planets*; the Prelude from *The Dream of Gerontius*; the second movement of Elgar's 2nd Symphony; the *Benedictus* by Mackenzie; *The Dead March in Saul*; *Solemn Melody*; and Sullivan's Overture *In Memorium.*

A concert was presented by the City of Birmingham Symphony Orchestra under Zubin Mehta on 21st October 1969 to commemorate the centenary of the birth of Mahatma Gandhi. Ravi Shankar and Yehudi Menuhin played a duet and a large Indian choir sang hymns particularly notable to unaccustomed ears by the tinkle of bells running through them. The Prince of Wales and Earl Mountbatten of Burma spoke to the assembly which included the Prime Minister, Harold Wilson, a number of other prominent politicians and many from the diplomatic corps.

1977 was the 150th anniversary of Beethoven's death and in commemoration the *Missa Solemnis* was performed in aid of the Spastics Society on 26th March by the New Philharmonia Orchestra, the London Choral Society and the Oriano Choir. One of the soloists, Pauline Tinsley, became too ill to carry on and from about the half way stage she gave way to a 28-year-old infant school teacher from Heston, Julia Dewhurst, who was a member of the London Choral Society; she received a standing ovation and the conductor summed up everyone's feelings when he said, ''Julia was absolutely wonderful. She did not put a foot wrong and very deservedly got a tremendous reception.''

Happily celebratory concerts far exceed the memorial ones and it is difficult to know which to include and which to leave out but space is available for only a few that may be taken as typical. The Hall was decorated with red, white and blue bunting and 60 Union Jacks for an Empire Day Concert, which for some unkown reason was held five days later on 29th May 1909. The artistes were all from different parts of the Empire, one of them being Emma Albani from Canada who contributed *Home, Sweet Home*. For many decades 24th May was always celebrated with members of the Royal Family attending a concert in honour of Empire Day. Naturally the programme content was designed to enhance the patriotic fervour which such an occasion demanded with orchestra or band, organ, massive choir and soloists. In 1938 the King and Queen were present when the youthful David Willcocks sang in the choir under Sargent. This was really the start of Sir David's long association with the Hall and he recalls seeing the Master of the King's Music, Sir Walford Davies, joining Princesses Elizabeth and Margaret Rose in the Royal Box for the afternoon rehearsal. Princess Elizabeth was with her parents at the 1945 concert organised jointly by the Empire Day Movement and the *Sunday Empire News.* As the war in Europe had been over less than three weeks the programme, fittingly, was presented by various services' bands. Sadly Empire Day has passed into history and the patriotic Royal occasions associated with it are no more.

The Coronation of George V in 1911 was celebrated on 22nd June in a rather curious fashion since of the three soloists only one was British, Edmund Burke of the Covent Garden Opera Company; the others were Elizabeth Von Endert and Guido Ciccolini, respectively of the Berlin and Paris Opera Companies.

The following year Sir Henry Wood celebrated his Golden Jubilee as an orchestral conductor on 5th October. He had conducted professionally for the first time on New Year's Day, 1888 and at the concert to acknowledge the milestone he was in charge of the first performance of a work specially composed for the occasion—Vaughan Williams' *Serenade to Music*. The L.S., L.P., and B.B.C. Symphony Orchestras with the Royal and B.B.C. Choral Societies and the Philharmonia Choir were joined on the platform by sixteen of the best-loved soloists of the time and what a splendid team they made—Isobel Baillie, Lilian Stiles-Allen, Elsie Suddaby, Eva Turner, Margaret Balfour, Muriel Brunskill, Astra Desmond, Mary Jarred, Parry Jones, Heddle Nash, Frank Titterton, Walter Widdup, Norman Allin, Robert Easton, Roy Henderson and Harold Williams. There was one other soloist at this memorable concert, none other than Sergei Rachmaninov who played his own Second Piano Concerto. The proceeds of this concert were donated as an endowment for beds in London Hospitals for the benefit of orchestral musicians.

Sir Henry was again at the centre of events on 25th March 1944 when his 75th birthday was celebrated jointly with the Golden Jubilee of his association with the Proms. The concert was arranged and presented by the *Daily Telegraph*, and Lord Camrose paid tribute to Sir Henry before a capacity audience which included the Queen and the Princesses Elizabeth and Margaret Rose. Solomon was the soloist in Beethoven's 3rd Piano Concerto and the B.B.C. Symphony , the L.S. and the L.P.Os. were conducted in turn by Boult, Sargent and Cameron, Sir Henry himself taking over the baton for the Overture, *The Flying Dutchman.*

1951 was Festival of Britain year during which the centenary of the Great Exhibition was celebrated with a wide variety of activities all over the country. As the Royal Albert Hall is a child of the Great Exhibition it was only natural and right that it should play a prominent role in the nation's celebrations. These encompassed the National Brass Band Clubs' Festival of Great Britain Concert; the Festival of Britain Concert given by the Philharmonia Orchestra under Raphael Kubelik with Yehudi and Hephzibah Menuhin as soloists in an all Brahms programme; and exclusive engagement of Vladimir Horowitz; Fürtwängler directing the Philharmonia Orchestra; and delightful entertainment by the ever popular Vienna Boy's Choir; and a memorable performance of Verdi's *Requiem* by the Teatra alla Scala Company directed by Victor De Sabata.

In 1964 the Duke of Edinburgh was present at Henry Wood's birthday concert rehearsal on 4th March, so .following the example of King Paul of Greece, Queen Frederica and the Princesses Sophia and Irene who had been there on 2nd March 1961. The Duke heard an orchestra of 300 and a choir of 700, drawn once again from the four principal London Schools of Music, rehearse the *Grande Messe des Morts* conducted by Sargent, with the famous Berlioz requirement of four brass bands positioned two on each side, one above the other in Boxes. The soloist was Gerald English.

The Royal College of Organists centenary was celebrated on 24th

September 1966 by a number of virtuosos putting the mighty organ through its paces; they included Aprahamian, Birch, Blades, Bower, Downes, Jackson, Neary, Preston, Gillian Weir, Westrup, Wicks and Willcocks.

Four Russian soloists entertained an audience which included the Soviet Ambassador, Mr Smirnovsky, Lords Boothby, Collison and Wade and the M.P., Renee Short when the Golden Jubilee of the Revolution was celebrated on 22nd October 1967.

The concert in aid of the Royal Albert Hall Centenary Appeal was a splendid Royal occasion taking place on 2nd April 1971 in the presence of the Queen; the Queen Mother; the Prime Minister, Edward Heath; the Leader of the Opposition, Harold Wilson and Mrs Wilson; the Leader of the Liberal Party, Jeremy Thorpe; the Lord Mayor of London and the Lady Mayoress; the Bishop of London, Dr Robert Stopford; Lord Redcliffe-Maud and some 200 other invited guests. They attended a reception in the Gallery and Mr Heath recalled he had

The centenary concert held in the Hall in 1971. *Royal Albert Hall*

not been up there since his student days. The L.S.O. under Pritchard played the Overture, *Cockaigne* and Rimsky-Korsakov's *Sheherazade*; Tchaikovsky's 1st Piano Concerto with John Lill and Bruch's 1st Violin Concerto with Alfredo Campoli. The lengthy programme also included Walton's *Belshazzar's Feast* conducted by the composer with the B.B.C. Choral Society, the R.C.S. and John Shirley-Quirk. To add to the gaiety a lot of Promenaders decked out in splendiferous Victoriana were present. This occasion was also the time the Queen unveiled a plaque in the Foyer commemorating the first hundred years of the Hall's history and the Prime Minister was presented with a bound copy of the *Jubilate* composed by Prince Albert.

Two years later Britain joined the European Economic Community (E.E.C.) and in celebration the Berlin Philharmonic Orchestra paid a 24 hours visit to London and played Beethoven's 4th and 5th Symphonies under Karajan.

In 1976 the famous Bach Choir became a centenarian and on 26th April with the Thames Chamber Orchestra, Heather Harper, Janet Baker, Robert Tear and John Shirley-Quirk gave a performance of the Mass in B Minor conducted by its Musical Director, David Willcocks, in the presence of the Queen Mother.

Concerts of one sort or another easily top the list as money makers so far as charities are concerned and many hundreds must have been promoted by scores of charitable organisations. It is impossible to give more than a sample in a book of this size, indeed they well might fill a whole volume if they were given full coverage. Some of them, more or less selected at random, have been chosen as representative of the wide scope of the talents they have brought to the platform of the Hall over a long period of time and the amazing variety of organisations that promoted them for a remarkable range of beneficent causes. Some are reasonably well documented yet others receive only the briefest of mentions in the records.

One of the earliest records is of a recital by John McCormack on 4th February 1909 in aid of an unspecified Italian disaster but things really got into their stride during the First World War. This naturally enough sparked off a great outburst of patriotic fervour and a period of immense charitable endeavour.

On 24th October 1914 there was a concert sponsored by the Grand Priory of the Order of the Hospital of St John of Jerusalem in England in aid of its European War Fund. The Queen's Hall Orchestra was conducted by Sir Henry Wood, the Massed Bands of the Brigade of Guards by Capt. J. Mackenzie-Hogan and the R.C.S. by Sir Frederick Bridge. H. L. Balfour was at the organ, F. A. Sewell was the accompanist and the soloists were Patti, Madame Edvina of the Royal Opera, a Japanese prima donna, Madame Muira, a boy soprano, Charles Mott, and Carrie Tubb, Phyllis Lett and Plunkett Greene. The Belgian, British, French, Japanese and Russian national anthems were played followed by the usual mélange of items so popular at the time.

Six weeks later on 6th December there was a Grand Patriotic Concert for Belgian Refugees; it was organised by a Madam Zizinia and like its predecessor commenced with the playing of the allied national anthems; the programme content was, however, much more classical.

Belgium's Independence Day was celebrated on 21st July 1916 when the audience was addressed by the Prime Minister, Herbert Henry Asquith, a Belgian Government Minister and a Member of the Chamber of Representatives prior to a recital by Clara Butt and two fine Belgian players—Eugene Ysäye (violin) and Arthur De Greef (piano). Later in the year and nearly two years before the end of hostilities a Grand Patriotic Concert in Thanksgiving for Victories by Land, Sea and Air was held on 16th December.

The organ as a solo instrument was used to help the war effort on 22nd October 1917 when H. L. Balfour gave a recital at a War Savings Meeting addressed by Lloyd George and Bonar Law under the Chairmanship of Sir Robert Kindersley. Then four months before the war ended an orchestra of 119 Belgian soldiers was sent from the continent by the Queen of the Belgians to give a Tribute to Britain Grand Concert; this was on 10th July 1918 and the soloists were Madame D'Alvarez and Robert Radford, and Lord Curzon spoke on the Glory of Belgium.

Haig's British Legion appeal for ex-servicemen was the recipient of the proceeds of a performance of John Herbert Fould's newly composed *World Requiem*; a work requiring enormous forces, it was given its premiere on 11th November 1924 by the R.P.O., the oddly named London Cenotaph Choir and Ida Cooper, Olga Haley, Herbert Heyer and William Heseltine. It is a pity the work is never performed nowadays because the Hall would provide a marvellous setting as it surely must have done nearly 60 years ago. Foulds was a 'cellist and a Mancunian and, like his father, was for a time a member of the Hallé Orchestra when Karl Richter was its conductor. It would be appropriate if some time in the not too distant future that fine orchestra could be prevailed upon to resurrect the composition of one of its players of the Edwardian era.

Ignacy Paderewski gave a recital of works by Bach, Mozart, Chopin and Liszt as well as himself in the presence of the King and Queen on 12th January 1933 in aid of the Musicians' Benevolent Fund. He was followed the next year by Conchita Supervia, Eva Turner and Richard Tauber giving a recital on 11th May on behalf of their less fortunate colleagues. This charity always seems to have been a firm favourite with the Royal Family and as each concert comes round it is certain some member, or members, will be present. The Queen Mother and the Duchess of Kent were there in 1972, the Queen Mother in 1974 and 1978, the Queen and Duke of Edinburgh in 1976 and Princess Alexandra and Angus Ogilvie in 1980. Every year the British orchestras take it in rotation to give their services on the Fund's behalf as do all the soloists; and the Royal Albert Hall and Royal Festival Hall take it turn about to stage these Royal

A Royal occasion, the concert in aid of the Royal Albert Hall Centenary Appeal on 2nd April 1971. *Royal Albert Hall*

Concerts which take place on, or close to, 22nd November, St Cecilia's Day, she being the patron saint of music. The 1972 concert was presented by the Royal Liverpool Philharmonic Orchestra conducted by Groves, the soloist being Craig Sheppard; they were followed by the R.P.O. under Raymond Leppard, the soloists being Sheila Armstrong and Shura Cherkassky. Then came the Scottish National Orchestra conducted by Alexander Gibson with Marisa Robles, James Galway and Paul Crossley, and the Hallé Orchestra directed by James Loughran with Steven Bishop-Kovacevich; and finally the City of Birmingham Symphony Orchestra under Simon Rattle with Emil Gilels.

Less than six months before the outbreak of the Second World War the British people were supporting the child victims of the Spanish Civil War when the L.S.O. under Albert Coates with the great Spanish 'cellist, Pablo Casals, performed.

Came the Second World War and with it a spate of performances on behalf of those directly involved. Three events in 1942 were typical. First, on 5th July,

King George's Fund for Sailors was the beneficiary of a concert given by the L.S.O. under Barbirolli with Parry Jones; in August there was a Celebrity Concert for the Fire Services Benevolent Fund and in November the L.S.O. conducted by Rudolph Dunbar with Cyril Smith played for the Colonial Comforts Fund. On 28th February 1945 a concert was given on behalf of the Children of Warsaw who had seen their city destroyed by the Nazis and then the rubble fought over by German and Russian forces; that any survived this fearful holocaust was miraculous, but survive they did, to be desperately in need of all possible aid that the Allies could give. Joan Cross, Mary McArthur, Peter Pears and Owen Brannigan joined the L.P.O., Leicester Philharmonic Society and Morley College Choir conducted by Basil Cameron in a programme which included Bax's *Fantasy on Polish Christmas Carols*, the Suite from the Ballet Pantomime *Harnasie* by Karol Szymanowski and Michael Tippett's Oratorio, *A Child of our Time*.

The termination of the war in Europe was the reason for a Victory celebration Concert on 31 May 1945 in aid of the Airborne Forces Security Fund at which Charles Münch conducted the L.P.O. in the presence of the Ambassadors of Belgium, Chile, China, Czechoslovakia, Denmark, France, the Netherlands, Norway and Poland and the Ministers of Ethiopia and Syria.

In the Autumn of 1946 the Berlin P.O. under its Principal Conductor, Sergiu Celibidache, played on behalf of Christian Action during its first visit to Britain since the end of the war. This was followed on 20th November by the L.S.O. conducted by Walter Goehr with Luigi Infantino playing and singing for the benefit of U.N.R.R.A. 1946 was also the year when the Hungarian violinist Tilmanyi gave a recital for Refugee Children's Welfare.

On 24th November 1947 the *Daily Telegraph* sponsored a concert on behalf of the British Empire Nurses' War Memorial Fund; it was given by the R.P.O. under Beecham with Kirsten Flagstad and Set Svandholm.

On 10th June 1963 the Freedom from Hunger Campaign was the recipient of the proceeds from the Army's biggest military band concert. Boult conducted 350 players of the Massed Bands of the Household Brigade supported by State Trumpeters and a Corps of Drums, Highland dancers from the Scots Guards, pipers from the Irish Guards and a choir from the Welsh Guards.

In August 1968 the United Nations Association and the Kubelik Foundation to aid Czech students stranded abroad, as a result of the Warsaw Pact invasion of Czechoslovakia, were the joint beneficiaries of a concert by the L.S.O. conducted by Daniel Barenboim with his wife, Jacqueline du Pré, the soloist in Dvořák's 'Cello Concerto. By an irony of timing that same night on the other side of London the U.S.S.R. State Symphony Orchestra and Svyatoslav Richter were playing in the Royal Festival Hall.

In 1950 the Vellore concerts were founded and have been held regularly ever since in support of the Vellore Christian Medical College and Hospital founded in 1900 in the small town of the same name some 75 miles from Madras. Today the Hospital is one of the world's great centres of healing, teaching and evangelism and is noted for its work on behalf of poliomyelitis sufferers. When the 1967 concert was given on 25th April a number of those afflicted with the disease were taken to the Hall by ambulance from West Hendon Hospital with police outriders ensuring a quick journey. The patients took with them their breathing apparatus, for which special power lines had been laid at the Hall.

An unusual event in 1948 was a National Savings Concert on 24th February. Nothing was spared in putting on an excellent performance presented by stars of great popularity. The L.S.O. and B.B.C. Choral Society were conducted by Leslie Woodgate and Arnold Greir was at the organ. The soloists were Alfredo Campoli, Anne Ziegler and Webster Booth, and Sadlers Wells Ballet performed excerpts from its repertoire. The finalists of the All-London Silver Lining £500 Talent Search were introduced by Jack Warner; there was a dramatic narrative entitled *The Challenge* and speeches from the Chancellor of the Exchequor, Sir Stafford Cripps, and the Chairman of the National Savings Movement, Lord Mackintosh of Halifax. To close the proceedings there was an epilogue by John Mills.

As we have seen already many famous composers, both native and foreign, have conducted their own works in the Hall but there are still two more that must be mentioned. Richard Strauss made his first appearance in London in 1897 and conducted the L.S.O. in a programme of his own works in the Hall on 15th January 1911 which he did again in 1947 with the Philharmonia Orchestra. The following year he returned to conduct his last concert at the Hall. Included in the programme was the *Domestic Symphony* which requires four saxhorns; as Strauss had written "Sax." for short it was open to wide interpretation and he was astonished, not to say displeased, when confronted by four saxophonists (soprano, alto, tenor, and baritone) specially engaged for the performance. At the end of 1954 Aram Khachaturian conducted the Philharmonia Orchestra in a programme of his own compositions, including the Suite from the Ballet *Gayaneh* and the Piano Concerto, with Moura Lympany playing the solo part. Just over 23 years later on 21st January 1977, he returned to conduct his last concert in the Hall; the L.S.O. played the 2nd Symphony and excerpts from *Gayaneh* and *Spartacus* and were joined by Nicholai Petrov for the Piano Concerto.

An innovation in 1953 was the launching by the L.P.O. of a project which proved most successful in introducing thousands of people to the classical repertoire at nominal cost. These so-called Industrial Concerts aim to provide popular music at the lowest possible price and each series consists of six concerts, some of which are repeated, depending on demand, given usually on Friday evenings during the Autumn and Winter. Tickets are sold on a group basis, each group having an organiser who makes all the arrangements for distributing advertising material, obtaining tickets and laying on transport. As the name implies the scheme's original concept was to appeal to workers on the shop floor but now its scope has widened to encompass schools, youth associations, church groups, white collar organisations and indeed any interested body of people. Since 1974 the concerts have been called Classics for Pleasure due to a recording company trading under that name taking over sponsorship; help is also received from the Greater London Council, the Arts Council and the London Orchestral Concert Board. All seats are disposed of at one price, each group receiving allocations in different parts of the Hall. The orchestral management liaises with groups by means of a committee of group organisers so that both parties are able to share each other's opinions and suggestions at regular intervals.

The L.P.O. also looks after its own interests by organising an annual concert in aid of its National Appeal Fund which is concerned with improving working conditions and consolidating security of employment. At many of these performances the Orchestra "relaxes" aided and abetted in recent years by entertainers of the calibre of Tony Bennett, Victor Borge, Duke Ellington and Danny Kaye. In February 1966 Kaye conducted the Orchestra and helped to raise about £10,000 for the Fund. Tickets cost up to fifty guineas (£52.50) each and included a champagne supper in the Balcony Restaurant with Princess Margaret, Peter Sellers and the conductor. The actual performance must have been quite hilarious as Kaye, with the cooperation of the Orchestra, gave a portrait gallery of "emotionally unstable" conductors; "you know the pram-pushers, the coffee-grinders, and the very excitable guy who plays it like it was the last piece in the world." Borge, apart from being a popular humourist, is no mean conductor and pianist and on 10th March 1974 he demonstrated his ability in both roles. He directed the Orchestra in the Overture, *Die Fledermaus*, Svendsen's *Romance in G* and excerpts from Gounod's *Romeo and Juliet* and then joined it to play Gershwin's Piano Concerto. The Fund is not always reliant on "funny men" and frolicsome programme material, however, and the 1980 event on 14th December was devoted to a performance of *Messiah* conducted by John Aldis and with Helen Walker, Alfreda Hodgson, Philip Langridge and David Thomas.

Wit and humour were of course the stock in trade of the much lamented Gerard Hoffnung, who apart from being an artist and raconteur of some repute was also an accomplished tuba player. He founded the Hoffnung Musical Festivals at which various witty musical parodies were performed and one of these was both broadcast and televised by the B.B.C. from the Hall on 18th December 1976; although that was long after Hoffnung's death in 1959 his creations are still resurrected from time to time.

One of the special concerts performed in 1982 was a celebration of Sir William Walton's eightieth birthday, in which the Trinity College of Music Orchestra, the Royal Choral Society and the Leeds Philharmonic Choir performed *Belshazzar's Feast*, with Manoug Parikian, violin, and Benjamin Luxon, baritone. Sir William did not long survive his birthday, for he died in March 1983.

In the same month as the Walton celebration, November, Mahler's Symphony No. 8 was performed by the Royal College of Music Symphony Orchestra supported vocally by the Royal College of Music Chorus, the Cambridge University Musical Society Chorus and the Royal College of Music Junior Department Chorus. Earlier in the year the Commonwealth Philharmonic Orchestra had played a largely Polish programme under the baton of Michael Bialoguski, with Fou T'song as the pianist. The Vienna Philharmonic under their eminent conductor Eugen Jochum were visitors in March that year, playing a Beethoven and Mozart programme. Beethoven, plus Elgar, Britten and Cox, featured in a concert given by the B.B.C Symphony Orchestra in the same month to commemorate the fiftieth anniversary of the B.B.C. External Services.

''One Arabian Night'' at the Royal Albert Hall on 17th November 1967. *Royal Albert Hall*

The most prestigious of many Royal Gala Concerts held over the years must have been that in April 1982 when the Italian opera singer Luciano Pavaroti, supported by the Royal Philharmonic Orchestra, gave a programme of operatic arias and Neapolitan love songs.

A recent innovation—it started in 1974—is the annual performance of a great choral masterpiece by amateur players and singers, who each, in exchange for a modest entry fee, can join with hundreds of other enthusiasts in demonstrating their talents. ''Music from Scratch'' was the brainchild of four scientists—Professor Reginald Garton and Drs David Burgess, Donald Munro and Gavin Park—and they chose *Messiah* as their first tentative production. The seeds were sown by Burgess and Monro but they were joined quickly by the others and so good was the organisation and publicity that by the time the great evening arrived some 2,500 singers and nearly 250 instrumentalists were assembled; as the B.B.C. had decided to televise the event the performance was seen by an even greater audience than originally anticipated and the cameras were helpful in providing free publicity for the years ahead. That this was an undoubted success story was due largely to the full commitment of the organisers since Park conducted, Burgess and Monro played in the orchestra and Garton was the backstage man. Since those heady days of 1974 ''Music from

The New Philharmonic Orchestra, conducted by Vilem Tausky, playing with the bands of the Welsh Guards and the Coldstream Guards. *Lauri Tjurin*

Scratch'' has not only changed its name to the ''Tuesday Partnership'' but broadened its repertoire to include such works as *Elijah* and the Brahms, Mozart and Verdi *Requiems* and there seems little doubt that the impulses of the ''scientific four'' have caught the imagination of performers and audiences alike.

The year 1982 saw two operatic music firsts, with the Tuesday Partnership in co-operation with the D'Oyly Carte Opera Company presenting *H.M.S. Pinafore from Scratch* and in October a world record being set for the largest choir ever to sing Gilbert and Sullivan. Richard Dickins was the conductor for *H.M.S. Pinafore from Scratch*, which featured Vivian Tierney, Meston Reid, Alistair Donkin, Gareth Jones, Catherine Wyn-Jones and John Ayldon. The record-breaking concert six months later, ''Gilbert and Sullivan's Greatest Hits,'' brought to the stage Marcus Dods conducting the Hertfordshire County Youth Orchestra and massed choirs led by the Royal Choral Society.

The year after ''Music from Scratch'' was launched the *Times Educational Supplement* initiated the Schools Prom, an event which brings together representatives of school groups from all over the country. The organisational work involved in such a project is formidable and from beginning to end takes something like six months, presenting the selection panels with the most difficult of tasks as they struggle to whittle down the potential participants to about 1,000—a sufficiently manageable number to squeeze into the Hall and ensure a wide spectrum of musical taste. Taste covers a multitude of possibilities ranging from full scale orchestras to brass, jazz and steel bands and from brass and percussion ensembles to handbell ringers and early music groups, but all are covered by the qualities of enthusiasm and talent displayed by the young performers. Guest groups from abroad are being invited and now many of the country's leading commercial enterprises are giving their financial backing, the visitors in 1980 being a choir from France.

The Schools Proms stemmed from the National Festival of Music for Youth held each year in August and supported by many famous musicians including Leopold Stokowski, who conducted a gala concert in 1973. The former Prime Minister, Edward Heath did much to establish and encourage the European Community Youth Orchestra and has conducted it on occasion both at home and abroad. For instance he and Lorin Maazel conducted it on 6th August 1978 when the programme included *A Young Person's Guide to the Orchestra*; the Prelude to Act 3 of *La Traviata*; the *Academic Festival Overture* and the *Symphonie Fantastique*. Although only a creation of the late 1970s it has already appeared to much acclaim in the Hall as has the much longer established National Youth Orchestra of Great Britain. In August 1977 there was an International Festival of Youth Orchestras and Performing Arts to which youth orchestras came from all over the world. The National Youth Marching Band Championships are staged annually.

Members of the Georgian State Dance Company perform for the photographers against the backdrop of a grimy Royal Albert Hall. *Royal Albert Hall*

Other young persons' concerts have been given by the London Schools' Music Association on 23rd June 1953 when the Duchess of Gloucester was present, and at the Staffordshire Schools' Music Festival held in June 1978.

Young people are again the centre of attraction at another favourite event which confirms its popularity each year by the substantial audience it draws. The Family Carol Concert organised by the Bach Choir is presented and conducted by its Musical Director, Sir David Willcocks, who has the happy knack of bringing to the occasion the family as well as the seasonal spirit. The children are always heavily involved, not only in the singing but also as participants in the conductor's "Quiz Time" and, a little more seriously, the winners of the year's carol competition are presented with their prizes and hear their compositions performed by the Choir.

Carols are of course just about everybody's favourites and this is reflected in the number of performances during the run-up to Christmas each year. In addition to the Bach Choir other regular organisers are the L.P.O., the Alexandra Choir and the London and Royal Choral Societies. Pre-Christmas performances of *Messiah* are also immensely popular and in this respect the L.P.O. and its famous chorus can be relied upon each year.

So far the last chapter and this one have been devoted to the Hall's role in the presentation of classical music but many other forms of musical entertainment have been presented over the years and cannot be overlooked because they have played a significant part in the history of the building.

For a number of years the National Brass Band Championships have attracted the finest works' bands in the country and the rivalry has been acute as many have come from Lancashire and Yorkshire and in some instances from towns very close to one another.

Military bands are also popular attractions frequently playing in their own right, in combination at massed band festivals and, as we have seen already, at big national affairs like the Festival of Remembrance and in association with orchestras. Every year the Massed Bands of the Royal Marines give a concert which is attended by members of the Royal Family.

From time to time the grace and excitement of Eastern European song and dance culture are brought to the Hall by such groups as the Czeckoslovakian State Song and Dance Ensemble; the Hungarian Gypsy Ensemble; the Romanian

Julia Romanenko and Nikolai Trubsky performing in the Hall during the visit of the Osipov Balalaika Orchestra in June 1968. *Royal Albert Hall*

Frank Sinatra arriving at the Royal Albert Hall in March 1977. *Lauri Tjurin*

State Rhapsody Orchestra and Ciocirlia Dancers; the Yugoslav National Singers and Dancers; the Majowsze Polish Song & Dance Company; and the Dagestan Dance Company from the Caucasus. From further afield but in the same style is the Yevshan Ukrainian Folk Ballet Ensemble from Saskatoon, Canada; and by way of contrast are Tony Praxmair and his Gay Tyrolese, the Baalbeck Dancers, the Sasono Milio Gamelin of Surakarta, Indonesia, and the Flamenco and Gitano Festival of 1965.

In November, 1959 the 60-member Georgian State Dance Company paid its first visit to England and amongst the audiences were the Soviet Ambassador, Jacob Malik, and Earl and Countess Mountbatten of Burma. ''Words cannot describe the fantastic wonders'' and ''These amazing dancers must be seen to be believed'' were the comments of a couple of newspaper critics. On 22nd September 1964 the 150-strong Moiseyav Dance Company had Zina Mikoyan, the daughter-in-law of the Chairman of the Soviet Council of Ministers, as one of its members and the performances included the Shake, the Hitch Hike and Twist in a coffee bar atmosphere of dark lights and loud music, the participants having Beatle haircuts. The final dance was a Mods and Rockers number in which guitars were played. Dame Margot Fonteyn was in the audience, which also included all the Russian Embassy staff.

On 9th June 1968 there was another fine attraction from the Soviet Union with the appearance of the Osipov Balalaika Orchestra and stars of the Bolshoi Opera and Ballet Company. The Orchestra is named after Nicholai Osipov, who was its conductor for five years from 1940, and is an ensemble of 65 musicians whose repertoire encompasses ancient folk and contemporary songs as well as adaptations of the works of the great Russian composers. The instruments used include six sizes of balalaika, the domra, which sounds something like a mandolin, the gusli, similar to a dulcimer, treshchoyki (rattles), the kugikli (flute), zhaleiki (pipes), Vladimir shepherds' horns, named after the area in Russia from which they originated, and accordians and harmonicas. This was a brilliant and sparkling entertainment with the artistes appearing in colourful national and stage costumes.

Since the Second World War several visits have been made by the Red Army Choir with an orchestra of accordians and balalaikas and a group of dancers also drawn from the army and totalling in all about 200 performers dressed in khaki jackets, blue trousers and jackboots.

Popular entertainers are of course legion, either as individuals or in groups, but all have their following. Of the solo performers perhaps the number one position must be given to Frank Sinatra who has appeared several times and on each occasion ensured a sell-out. Early in 1977 he gave eight performances in six days, with stout support from the 5th Dimension and Pat Henry, and probably

The new floor laid in 1934 has proved ideal for dancing, both recreational and competitive.
C. Christodoulou

could have gone on filling the Hall for several more days. His appearance on 29th May 1975 did, however, pose some problems because of a black market in tickets and 400 fans with forged tickets were turned away. As for the rest of the "populars" they are too numerous to record either as individuals or as groups or bands; suffice to say that it is unlikely there are any in the top bracket of either that has not appeared at some time or other.

A Latin American Dance Formation Team in action in the Royal Albert Hall. *C. Christodoulou*

On 6th April 1968 the Eurovision Song Contest was held, contestants being drawn from Austria, Belgium, Eire, Finland, France, Germany, Italy, Luxembourg, Monaco, Netherlands, Norway, Portugal, Spain, Sweden, Switzerland, United Kingdom and Yugoslavia.

Dancing has for long been a popular feature of activity in the Hall and it presents much diversity of style from ballroom to folk and Latin American. The principal annual events are the International Ballroom Championships and the English Folk Dance and Song Society Festival.

This chapter and the previous one have given some idea of the extraordinary depth of musical appreciation which has come to the Hall in a never failing stream but inevitably many names have had to be omitted for lack of space.

CHAPTER SEVEN

The Spectacle and the Pageantry

THROUGHOUT its historic hundred years the Royal Albert Hall has been the scene of many spectacular events, both happy and sombre, but none have been as moving as the annual Royal British Legion Festival of Remembrance which combines both these qualities in unique combination. The change of mood from sheer pageantry and joyful enthusiasm and exuberance to one of religious remembrance and dedication is impressive indeed and yet does not seem in any way incongruous or misplaced even though the transition is made in the space of only a minute or two.

After the First World War the 11th November, the date when hostilities ceased, was declared the annual day of remembrance when the nation paid homage at the Cenotaph to those who had made the supreme sacrifice. In 1927 there was the usual service in Whitehall but this time it was followed in the evening by an ex-service reunion in the Royal Albert Hall, organised by Michael Wardell of the *Daily Express* working in conjunction with the British Legion. This was essentially a convivial gathering for sharing memories and experiences and the well known author and correspondent, H. V. Morton, commented that "There has never been anything like it in the history of reunion. Ten thousand Englishmen, bound by the mightiest memories of our time, met together to sing to the world the songs they sang in Hell." This nostalgic get-together was attended by the Prince of Wales, afterward Edward VIII and later Duke of Windsor, and after the festivities he led the entire company on a march to the Cenotaph. The following year the date fell on a Sunday and consquently the arrangements devolved largely into a Remembrance Service and so it was that the pattern of pageantry, entertainment and remembrance was quickly established which has prevailed ever since apart from four anniversaries during the Second World War. This time the occasion was honoured by the presence of George V and Queen Mary, the Duke and Duchess of York, who later became George VI and Queen Elizabeth, and Prince and Princess Arthur of Connaught.

1929 was the first year of the dual arrangement of secular and religious and was organised solely by the British Legion with the first part of the proceedings devoted to a pageant of Empire, a theme, alas, now completely outmoded and overtaken by events but in the heady days of 50 years ago utterly appropriate to the time. The second part of the event was given over to an act of remembrance, the culmination of which was the now familiar shower of poppies from the roof of the Hall, each one a silent witness and memory of a comrade who had not returned from the holocaust. The Prince of Wales attended the ceremony again in 1930 as Patron of the Legion accompanied by four Indian princes.

The interruption caused by the Second World War was terminated in 1943 when the Festival was held in the presence of George VI and Queen Elizabeth, the Duke and Duchess of Gloucester, the Duchess of Kent and the Deputy Prime Minister, Clement Attlee. In spite of wartime exigencies 180 branches of the Legion were represented as well as many active service men and women and the theme was the predictable one of "the fight for freedom." Civil Defence was well represented and the service was conducted by the Dean and Chapter of Westminster with the Abbey Choir.

For the past 10 years the Bishop of London has conducted the service, succeeding the Bishop of Birmingham, the Rt. Rev. John Leonard Wilson, who had experienced personally the horrors of war in the Far East, having been captured by the Japanese at the fall of Singapore. He had participated in the service for many years prior to his death in 1970 and he it was who succinctly summed up the significance of it all with the words "At that service

Left: The Royal Air Force Queen's Colour Squadron continuity drill team at the 1982 Festival of Remembrance.

Opposite: The Queen and the Duke of Edinburgh with other members of the Royal Family at the 1982 Festival.
C. Christodoulou

we thank God for men and women of all nations and of every age who have suffered or given their lives for truth and freedom.'' So great is the demand for tickets, which are never on sale to the public but are allocated through the Legion's branches, that a Saturday afternoon production is staged in addition to the well known one of the evening, which is always attended by several members of the Royal Family, including the Queen and the Duke of Edinburgh if they are not prevented by illness or absence from the country. The 50th Anniversary Festival on 8th November 1980 was attended by the Prime Minister, Mrs Margaret Thatcher, and members of the Cabinet and Shadow Cabinet.

On New Year's Day, 1942 there was a Military Pageant of the Empire and Her Allies which served to demonstrate the unity of the allied nations as they strove to overcome the evil arrayed against them and also to demonstrate the powerful forces they were able to command in their fight against Fascist tyranny. The Pageant was held under the auspices of the Officers' Sunday Club and the music was provided by massed bands, the Trumpeters of the Royal Horse Guards, the Pipers of the Seaforth Highlanders of Canada and the organ. The allied nations represented were Belgium, China, Czechoslovakia, France,

Great Britain, Greece, Luxemburg, Netherlands, Norway, Poland, United States, the U.S.S.R. and Yugoslavia; there were contingents from the Dominions and Colonies, from the Women's Services and all branches of the Civil Defence and Nursing services. Addresses were given by the Archbishop of Canterbury, the Cardinal Archbishop of Westminster and Admiral Sir Edward Evans. Carols were sung by Czech and Polish Choirs and Tchaikovsky's Overture, *1812* concluded the proceedings.

This event was followed on St George's Day and the convenient synchronisation of Shakespeare's birthday by a *Daily Express* presentation of our glorious past, present and future entitled "Battle for Freedom." It was divided into sections depicting the Crusades; Wat Tyler's Rebellion; the Wars with France, perhaps in the circumstances a rather indelicate subject; the Elizabethan period; Cromwell's Commonwealth; Empire; Victoria's long reign; the First World War; the turbulent present of the Second World War; and a vision of the future. That same year on 3rd August, King Haakon VII celebrated his 70th birthday and his subjects presented a Festnote in their native language in his

Poppy petals, each one representing a life sacrificed in the service of this country, showering on participants in the 1982 Festival of Remembrance. *C. Christodoulou*

Countess Mountbatten of Burma, with Colonel the Viscount Slim and Lord Braborne, greeting a member of the Burma Star Association during a reunion.
C. Christodoulou

honour; the King was present at this tribute to the love and affection he had accumulated during his reign and of his wartime leadership after being driven out of his homeland by the invading German forces.

One of the best known of post-war get-togethers is the Alamein Reunion, the first of which was on 23rd October 1946 when the Desert Rats* were addressed by Winston Churchill, then Leader of the Opposition, and Field Marshal Viscount Montgomery of Alamein. A year later the same gathering was addressed once again by ''Monty'' accompanied this time by the Foreign Secretary, Ernest Bevin. The bands of the Welsh Guards and Royal Artillery played, there was community singing led by the ''Forces' Sweetheart'', Vera Lynn, and extracts from a film of the 8th Army's desert victory. To celebrate the 21st anniversary of the famous battle ''Monty'' was there as usual and with him on this special occasion on 23rd October 1963 were the Queen Mother, the Earl of Avon and Lieut. General Sir Oliver Leese; the entertainment was provided by Marlene Dietrich, Vera Lynn, and Bud Flanagan.

The Burma Star Reunion follows much the same pattern except for the speakers. In 1947 such well known personalities as Vera Lynn, Sophie Tucker,

*Soldiers from 7th Armoured Division whose divisional sign was a Desert Rat or Jerboa but often loosely applied to all British troops who fought in the desert Campaign, Middle East, Second World War.

Noel Coward, Leslie Henson and Elsie and Doris Waters appeared. On 1st June 1951 Earl Mountbatten of Burma and Field Marshal Sir William Slim addressed the gathering; the Duke of Edinburgh was present on 3rd June 1955, the Queen Mother on 29th April 1972 and 26th April 1980 and on 30th April 1977 Earl Mountbatten was accompanied by Princess Anne and Captain Mark Phillips and the High Commissioners of Burma, India, Nepal and Pakistan.

Lavish entertainment is commonplace at the Hall and has been so virtually from the beginning, as witness the spectacular events associated with the state visits of the Shah of Persia and the German Emperor in Victoria's time. Those were musical events attended by all the trappings and panoply of state occasions but for sheer extravaganza one has to look at the many balls which have frothed and sparkled in the Hall for a century. Originally the Arena was used for dancing and the seats not occupied by seatholders used for sitting out; the corridors and Gallery were convenient for conversation and strolling, and the Boxes ideal for small parties. In those early days the special floor did not exist and three decades were to elapse before this useful adjunct to the Hall's amenities became available.

On 11th July 1883 between four and five thousand revellers enjoyed themselves at the Savage Club Ball which set the standard for lavishness and extravagance which few since have equalled let alone excelled. The proceeds were in aid of the Royal College of Music and the Savages went all out for authenticity, the Red Indian costumes they wore being correct in every detail; members who had visited the Indian Reserves in the United States gave their counsel, the South Kensington Museum's collection of Indian clothing had been thoroughly examined, and clothes, ornaments and arms were loaned by Lords Dunraven and Castletown and others. One Savage is said to have carried reality to the limit by including genuine scalps in his apparel. There was a two-hour variety entertainment with a specially selected orchestra and music was also played by the bands of the Royal Horse Guards and the 6th Thuringian Regiment as well as by Coote and Jinney's, the Victorian equivalent of the famous dance bands of the inter-war years of this century; even the organ was played by a Savage in full regalia. Dancing went on until dawn, as many as 2,000 at a time being on the floor. Chief guests were the Prince and Princess of Wales, the Duke of Albany and the Princess of Saxe-Meiningen who were escorted to the Royal Box by 30 braves.

The first notable ball of the Edwardian era on 9th June 1903 was in aid of the London Hospital, an institution dear to the heart of Queen Alexandra and to which she devoted a considerable amount of her time and energy. Tickets were priced at one guinea (£1.05) but the black-market rate was ten guineas (£10.50). The president of the organising committee was the Countess of Derby and the glittering gathering of the aristocracy numbered 4,500. The main attraction of the evening was a set of nine fancy-dress quadrilles forming a series of international dances with the ladies in national costume and the men attired in red dress coats, black knee breeches and stockings and buckled shoes.

There can be little doubt that for sheer exotica, extravagance and opulence of display, exhibitionism and glorious fun little if anything can approach the Chelsea Arts Club Ball which consistently year after year maintained the highest level of those attributes which other organisers usually had to cope with only once and then never have to repeat. The Club was founded with a membership of 40 in 1890 by James Abbott McNeill Whistler and the beginnings of the ball were in the form of Mardi-Gras Carnivals in the wilds of Chelsea, organised by the hundreds of artists who frequented that august suburb of the capital. Informal high jinks in their studios eventually spilled over into the local Town Hall and then to Covent Garden of all places. Finally in 1910 the Ball was held for the first time in the Hall where it remained as an annual event, apart from the war years, until its demise in 1958. The date was eventually changed from Shrovetide to New Year's Eve and each Ball contributed handsomely to charity.

The carnival atmosphere was maintained by extravagant floats manned in many instances by gorgeous girls dressed in fantastic costumes or even without

The Chelsea Arts Ball, which was unrivalled for extravagance and fun until its demise in 1958.
Royal Albert Hall

costume at all; behaviour which provoked a lady to write to "The Department of Public Morals, the London County Council", complaining that "At a recent Gala New Year's Eve night at the Chelsea Arts Ball women were openly mixing with the throngs quite naked. I have always understood this sort of thing was an offence against the Law." Each year the Ball adopted a theme which the floats and many of those attending attempted to epitomise although any form of fancy dress constume, varied, beautiful and ingenious, was not frowned upon by the organisers and there were even those who preferred to appear in ordinary evening dress. The whole affair was topped off with a surfeit of decorations, spotlights, dancing to a well known band, food and drink, the latter often being the cause of unseemly behaviour by those with more money than sense, although there was nearly always a boorish element present delighting in making a disturbance of some sort or other. For all their possible slight moral deficiencies these Balls were obviously splendid occasions to the extent of inciting one observer of the 1911 event to comment that it was the "most wonderful thing of any kind held in London" and "the scene was a riot of colour enhanced by the glow of thousands of electric lamps".

At the Golden Jubilee, and last, Ball there occurred one of the most serious incidents ever to happen at the Hall when in the early hours of New Year's Day, 1959 a smoke bomb was detonated in one of the corridors on the West side of the building. The emission was very dense and blacked out parts in the vicinity of the explosion causing considerable discomfort to the revellers, thirteen of whom were overcome by the smoke and had to receive treatment in the Ambulance Room. The canister was of the practice gas bomb type and as such was covered by the Explosives Act. An individual was detained but the Metropolitan Police Legal Department came to the conclusion that despite considerable investigation there was not sufficient evidence to prosecute. The decision seems to have been based on two particular points. One of the principal witnesses, who had earlier identified from a photograph the man who was thought to be the culprit, subsequently refused to identify him in the presence of Police officers and in any case the suspect had emigrated to Australia.

If the Chelsea Arts Ball was the most flamboyant annual romp at the Hall there were several one time balls which must have been serious rivals. Two of the principal contenders occurred in the golden days before the First World War and there has probably been nothing quite like them since, for splendiferous opulence, apart possibly for the Coronation Balls of 1937 and 1953.

The 20th June 1911 was the date of a Shakespeare Ball held as part of the celebrations of George V's coronation which took place two days later. The organisers were able to cash in on this occasion of national rejoicing because nearly all the Royal Family was present. Some 80 members of foreign Royal houses and official representatives from many countries as well as the Prime Minister and his wife, and Winston Churchill, graced the event with their presence. The object of the exercise was to raise funds for the Shakespeare Memorial Theatre at Stratford-upon-Avon and souvenir booklets alone cost five guineas (£5.25) each. As befitted the occasion the Hall had been decorated to resemble something like the Warwickshire countryside garnished with aspects of Tudor times such as stuffed peacocks. The Loggia Boxes were adorned with yew trees clipped into shapes conmmensurate with the style of the Bard's day and above them the Grand Tier Boxes were transformed into vineclad bowers complete with bunches of grapes. The Second Tier resembled a stone colonnade broken at intervals by columns and vases and the Balcony had been converted into flower beds fronted by a sloping lawn; finally the Gallery, which was the buffet area, had its columns obscured by cypresses rising towards a "cloudless sky" of blue gauze suspended high up under the great dome. The organ was discreetly obscured by bushes, trees and other foliage as were the band players and even the red curtains of the Boxes had been replaced temporarily by green ones. For a time the dancing was interrupted by a presentation of quadrilles and tableaux representing various historical events and scenes from Shakespeare's plays; indeed virtually everyone present was dressed as a Shakespearian character —even the police, who were there in strength to protect not only the high ranking personages themselves but also their expensive possessions, were attired in appropriate garb as Iagos, Romeos et al and the soldiers on duty were in the uniforms of Elizabethan England. The press, of course, was there in force and one correspondent declared in his copy that "There were Romeos by the score, Juliets by the dozen, Lady Macbeth did the quadrille with Sir Walter Raleigh and Hamlet waltzed with a red-haired Portia. King Lear did a two-step with Cleopatra, and Mary Queen of Scots in rich red velvet, swirled round in the arms of Shylock".

Earlier in the evening, a State Banquet had been held at Buckingham Palace and this delayed the arrival of the important guests at the Hall until close on 11 p.m. The Royal Party—which did not include the King and Queen, who were too busy with Coronation preparations—entered the Hall together. They were led by the Duke and Duchess of Connaught, their son and daughter, Prince Arthur and Princess Patricia; the Crown Princes and Princesses of Sweden, Greece and Germany; and the Crown Princess of Roumania. A fanfare of trumpets heralded their arrival and progress towards the Royal boxes was accompanied by loud and prolonged applause. A policeman, dressed as a beef-eater, succinctly summed up the situation to a colleague as they leaned on their spears—"Must be a million pounds worth of jewellery here tonight. Only hope one or two slick-fingered gents we know aren't here as well".

Two months before Europe was plunged into the turmoil of war, the 100th Anniversary of Peace among English-speaking peoples was celebrated on 10th June 1914 by another lavish and spectacular ball. This time the Hall was decorated in red, white and blue with gold coats-of-arms and flower baskets.

The highlight, however, was the replica of Christopher Columbus' ship, *Santa Maria*, imposingly placed across the Hall in front of the organ; at midnight the main lights were dimmed and ''Columbus'' and two of his officers appeared on the poop illuminated by spotlights. Then there paraded in the Arena characters representative of the discovery of the New World—Red Indians, Sir Walter Raleigh, the Virginian settlers, the Pilgrim Fathers, William Penn and the Quakers, and the signatories of the 1814 Treaty; they were followed by Britannia and her entourage of 50 attendants representing Britain and a group of ladies from the United States symbolising the American part of the concordat.

When hostilities ceased at the end of 1918 there was a flurry of ''Ball'' activity—there was a Victory Ball on 27th November, the Friends of Italy Ball, the Chelsea Arts Club ''Peace Ball'', and United Services Ball on 29th January 1919 and the Three Arts Club Balls on 12th February 1919 and 12th May 1920. The Victory Ball was marred because Billie Carlton, a popular stage personality and at the time leading lady in the London production of *Hoop La*, was found dead in one of the Boxes.

Balls are not the cheapest of events to stage manage and it is interesting to recall the Happy New Year Ball of 1926 with its resulting financial implications; it is on record that the organisers engaged 120 musicians (a far greater number than in the average present day symphony orchestra) at a fee of £3 per head plus

Opposite: Year after year thousands of boys came to the Albert Hall for the festival "Boy Scout", this being the finale of the 1959 pageant.

Right: An Indian scene from a similar event in 1938.
The Scout Association

15/- (75p) per hour overtime; 20 firemen; 30 attendants; six detectives; four catering managers; and eight photographers and various organising and publicity staff. Comestibles included 125 gallons of coffee; 100 cases of wines; 1,000 mineral waters, 300 bottles of whisky, and 8,000 rolls. The beneficiaries of this expensive evening's entertainment were the British Empire League and the Middlesex Hospital.

Butlin's the holiday firm hold Butlin's Beavers, a reunion of children up to 12 years old, and no expense seems to have been spared. For instance in February 1954 the entertainment included a demonstration of precision marching by the Women's Royal Army Corps, the band of which provided the music; there were clowns, stilt walkers, a pantomime horse on roller skates; the Ballet Montmartre doing a spectacular acrobatic can-can; and a motor cyclist circling in a vast wheel held on human shoulders. To round off everything the children took part in square dancing.

The Festival of Britain in 1951 celebrating the centenary of the Great Exhibition had as one of its events a Miss World Contest which, at the time, it was never contemplated repeating. However, it proved so successful and was considered something of an international relations cementer that it became an annual event and has appeared in the Hall's calender since 1969. Television has brought this display of feminine beauty and charm into millions of homes all over the world and has the added piquancy of being competitive so that viewers are able to pit their skill in the selective process with the judges in the Hall, who are usually well known show business personalities. The originator of the contest was Eric Morley, then an executive of Mecca International Ltd., which has sponsored it ever since with Morley becoming chairman and his wife, Julia, chief executive of the organisation. All the proceeds are devoted to the Variety Club of Great Britain, the national body of Variety Clubs International which is the largest children's charity in the world, operating irrespective of colour, race or

Contestants in the Miss World contest parade before the judges in their national costumes.
C. Christodoulou

creed. The 1970 contest on 20th November was being compered by Bob Hope and had reached its final stages when it was disrupted by supporters of the Women's Liberation Movement aided and abetted by a group of Young Liberals. Tomatoes, bags of flour, leaflets, smoke and stink bombs were thrown and there were protests that the show was like a ''cattle market''. The police had to be called to assist the security staff to eject the screaming and struggling demonstrators from the Hall but in spite of the turmoil there were no injuries and little damage and eventually the contest ran its course. Earlier in the day a home-made bomb went off under a B.B.C. Outside Broadcast van but with no effect. It is said there is more security in operation for the Miss World Contests than for visits by the Royal Family but on this occasion its defences were breached and found wanting although generally all is good humoured and the girls themselves have been described as a ''jolly group''.

The diamond jubilee of the St John Ambulance service was celebrated in October 1982. The St John Cadet Spectacular staged on that occasion featured a massed choir of 500, pyrotechnic disco dancers, handbell ringers, massed gymnastics, a massed band of 100 players and community singing, and lastly an "1812 Paper Bag Overture".

St John Cadets form the cross of St John in the arena during the St John Cadet movement's diamond jubilee celebrations. *C. Christodoulou*

CHAPTER EIGHT

Religion

IN THE early years religion was, like politics, a subject that had to be avoided to comply with the charter requirements and it is perhaps somewhat ironic that one of the earliest problems facing the Council concerning these topics was one where there was a certain identity of interest. In 1882 the Shop Hours Labour League hired the Hall for a meeting without any objection from the Council, but a year later an application to hold another meeting was refused in the first instance, possibly because the matter of the number of hours shop assistants were expected to work had become a burning issue in the country and had brought the League into national controversy. From the unlikely quarter of Canterbury the League suddenly regained its respectability in the eyes of the Council when the Archbishop let it be known that he was willing to become a patron of the League; so on the principle that what is good enough for the Archbishop is good enough for the Council the application was reconsidered, subsequently granted and the meeting went off without disturbance. A political issue had become a non-political issue by the mere writing of a letter by the Primate, but by so doing he had not transgressed in the other direction by making the issue have religious connotations—at least so the Council viewed it, and that was all that mattered.

Religion's first real effort to break into the sanctity of the Hall occurred the following year and met with the predictable rebuff. In fact it may be wondered why the Earl of Aberdeen wasted his time in requesting the use of the Hall for the purpose of holding a service prior to the departure home to the United States of America of Dr Dwight Lyman Moody, who had been on an evangelising crusade in Britain. However, the worthy Dr Moody was redeemed in 1937 when the National Centenary Celebration of his birth was held in the Hall, chaired by the Marquess of Aberdeen and Temair.

Problems had arisen virtually as soon as the Hall had been opened and the Sunday organ recitals inaugurated. These brought immediate protests from the Lord's Day Observance Society, which, however, did not pursue the matter too strongly. Three years later the National Sunday League sold tickets for the concerts in advance and the Society threatened to bring down the law in retribution on the Council which decided that discretion was the better part of valour and abandoned the concerts. In 1877 they were restarted, ways and means having been found of circumventing the law and frustrating the Society at the same time. Three years passed and another series of concerts was started for the "deserving poor" with free entry for this underprivileged class, the effect of which was yet again to thwart the Society. The arrangement was that free entry entitled members of the audience to standing room only, those wishing to be seated having to pay threepence (1.25p), sixpence (2½p) or a shilling (5p), depending on the position. Surprisingly even with free admission and low seat prices the concerts made a profit. Sometimes the concerts took the form of straight organ recitals, at others a singer or two would join in and from time to time there would be an instrumentalist. Hundreds of these concerts were given and many thousands of people enjoyed them, no doubt much to the chagrin and dismay of the Society. In order for the Society to be put even further out of court the Council decided to obtain a licence designating the Hall a place of public worship. By 1891 everything was in order and the Society was finally defeated in its prohibitive intentions and the whole scheme was given royal respectability by no less a person than the Duke of Edinburgh, who was a talented musician himself as we have already seen, but who could hardly be classed as a member of "what is known as the lower middle-class and the well-to-do artisan population," the euphemistic description given to those for whom the concerts were instigated, though they were really recitals rather than concerts, at least by today's interpretation of the words.

In the Autumn of 1897 the National Temperance Council Conference was opened by the Archbishop of Canterbury and in direct opposition to the strident views of the Lord's Day Observance Society delegates took the view that Sunday concerts were a blessing in disguise since they helped to take people away from the evils of the bottle and would assist in easing the burden of those unfortunates who had to work on the Sabbath making and dispensing abominable liquor. So Sunday music making could be described fairly as being one man's meat and another man's poison.

In February 1905 something new in religious fervour came to the Hall in the form of a two-man team from the United States which went under the name of the Torrey-Alexander Mission. It came to England with an established evangelising reputation and held 85 consecutive meetings, large numbers being turned away on each occasion, and attracting onto the platform several notabilities to give support including the Chaplain-General to the Forces.

If the Torrey-Alexander Mission was somewhat bizarre and rather ahead of its time even more so were the events on Easter Monday, 1928 when the Elim Evangel of the Foursquare Gospel held a mass baptism in the Hall as the culmination of a series of revivalist meetings held up and down the country. This strangely named sect had been formed twelve years previously in the Eirean town of Monaghan by a Welshman named George Jeffreys and the climax of each meeting he held was when the converts were baptised. In order to enable this to happen special arrangements had to be put in hand for the immersions in a stream of water supposedly representing the River Jordan. The paraphernalia required for the "Jordan" consisted of a purpose-made galvanised iron tank through which a stream of water was directed. The tank was placed on the stage and surrounded by sand, the whole being floodlit and camouflaged with banks of flowers. Access to the water was by a flight of steps at each side with a man in grey flannel trousers and white shirt stationed alongside to assist the converts make their entries and exits, while in the middle of the tank stood the black gowned Jeffreys performing the ceremony. The converts changed into suitable clothing in the Artistes and Choir Rooms and when they appeared in the Auditorium the females were dressed in white robes and shoes and the males in white shirts and shorts. There was a choir of some 2,000 young people called Crusaders, which sang hymns at appropriate places and Jeffreys preached a sermon. For a number of years the Elim Evangel has held regular Easter conferences, meetings and rallies in the Hall. As far back as 1937 the Campaign Hymns used in "Principal George Jeffreys' Revival and Healing Campaigns" were the major attraction and the Diamond Jubilee Celebrations in 1975 were based on the testimony that "We believe in the Bible from Cover to Cover" with special reference to Matthew I, 21 (Saviour); Matthew VIII, 17 (Healer); John I, 33 (Baptism) and I Thessalonians, IV, 16, (Coming King).

Prior to the appearance of Jeffreys and his Crusaders there had been another invasion from the United States but it was a far different manifestation from that provided by Torrey and Alexander. In the 1920s and 1930s America was in the throes of what came to be known as "Hot-gospelling", its exponents being predominantly negroes acting either as individuals or in small groups as they attempted to propagate and spread the Word of the Lord in the idiom of the period. As jazz and the negro spiritual were all the rage this was the form used by the gospellers and one such, Aimée McPherson, made an appearance in the Hall when this particular form of evangelism was at the height of its popularity on the other side of the Atlantic though it never caught on in Britain. Billy Graham is with little doubt the best known of modern evangelists and he has used the Hall on several occasions for his missionary work, in 1981 being given popular support by Cliff Richard.

Music, of course, plays a big part in worship and the Royal School of Church Music is very much the leader in this respect and receives well merited support from the Royal Family from time to time. On 6th June 1951 Princess Elizabeth attended a performance, as she did as Queen on 25th June 1970 whilst the Queen Mother was present on 10th May 1958 and at the Golden Jubilee Festival on 30th June 1977.

A correlation of music is the play, especially the pageant play, and this was introduced in a novel way in April 1927 when the United Society for the Propagation of the Gospel recounted its history from 1701-1927 in a pageant entitled "The Call of the World" which was repeated and brought up to date eight years later under the title of "From Sea to Sea". The year afterwards a

Five hundred Salvation Army cadets at their commissioning in 1932. *B.B.C. Hulton Picture Library*

company called The Grael presented *The Hound of Heaven* by F. Thompson in which there were 1,200 performers, young and old.

The propagation of the value of scripture reading and prayer has figured prominently in Christian endeavour and for four organisations in particular. The Bible Testimony Fellowship met in 1927 and 1930 "To affirm belief in the full inspiration of the Word of God and great evangelical doctrines" and in 1932 staged a Great Bible Demonstration. Its peak moment surely must have been on 27th November 1938 when the Emperor of Ethiopia, Haile Selassie, then in exile due to the invasion of his country by the Italians, gave his Bible testimony. The International Bible Reading Association and the League of Prayer and Service have held meetings in the Hall and the Scripture Union celebrated its Diamond Jubilee in 1939. Following the publication of the Good News Bible the Bible Society organised in the Spring of 1980 an unusual competition called "Sing Good News" in celebration of the occasion. Selwyn

Hughes founded the Crusade for World Revival in 1965 an interdenominational organisation to encourage people to spend time daily in prayer and bible reading; in a short time it has achieved considerable success and its following is already large enough to warrant the holding of an annual rally in the Hall.

The termination of the First World War drew a gathering of another kind when the King and Queen and the Prince of Wales attended a Thanksgiving Service organised by the Free Churches, which also called for a programme of international disarmament on 27th February 1928, a call, alas, which went unheeded and is still ignored today. That same year Christian internationalism was the theme of speeches by Sir Samuel Hoare and the Bishop of Manchester at the Anglo-Catholic Congress Anniversary of the Society of St Peter and St Paul. There was another impressive assembly on 7th February 1949 when 7,000 Roman Catholics led by 15 Archbishops and Bishops packed the Hall to protest at the detention and trial of the Primate of Hungary, Cardinal Jozef Mindszenty, who had been convicted of treason by the Communist government in Budapest and sentenced to life imprisonment. Among the speakers was the Archbishop of Liverpool, and many peers, M.P.s, priests, nuns and even peasant refugees were present and hundreds more were turned away because the Hall was full.

About the same number of Roman Catholics met in the Hall on 10th February 1958 for a Lourdes Centenary Festival commemorating the first occasion that Bernadette Soubirous saw the vision of the Blessed Virgin near the grotto. Those present included the Lord Mayor of London, the Archbishop of Westminster, the Bishop of Brentwood and the Apostolic Delegate, Archbishop O'Hara, who gave the blessing at the conclusion of a programme which was both grave and gay. Eamonn Andrews told Irish stories; Père Aimé Duval sang and played the guitar, Edmund Rubbra's *Cantata in Honorem Marial Matris Dei* was sung by Sylvia Fisher, Constance Shacklock and a choir of 500 convent schoolgirls, with Dom Gregory Murray of Downside Abbey at the organ; and Hugh Ross Williamson's *The Mime of Bernadette*, a combination of drama and poetry, was performed.

The Salvation Army has a long association with the Royal Albert Hall, the first occasion being on 11th March 1895 when a great rally was held to welcome home the Army's Founder, General William Booth, who had been on an exhausting six months' tour of Canada and the United States, during which he had addressed over 300 meetings attended by some half a million people. Not only was the Hall packed to the doors but there was a band of some 350 players and a choir of a thousand, not forgetting the organ. Groups representing different aspects of the Army's activities presented addresses of welcome on the platform and then the General spoke to the throng about his travels illustrating his points with limelight illuminated pictures effectively "blown-up" to be seen all over the Hall. Booth must have been the possessor of a stentorian voice because it is recorded that he spoke without the aid of a microphone and yet was audible virtually throughout the vastness of the Hall. Proceedings concluded with a commissioning ceremony for those about to leave for the far corners of the earth to perform their evangelistic work.

Just over eight years later Booth was at the Hall again after completing yet another mission to Canada and the United States. This tour's welcome home was on 30th March 1903 and was attended by David Lloyd George and another packed assembly which heard of the General's visit to the White House, where he had been received by President Theodore Roosevelt, and of him leading the prayers in the Senate. Three months after the latest homecoming Booth was received by Edward VII at Buckingham Palace on 24th June and later was at the opening in the Hall of the third International Congress at which he welcomed 8,000 delegates from all over the world. A fortnight later the closing ceremony was held in the Hall, the culmination of a series of meetings in different parts of the capital. Among those present were the Bishop of Hereford, the Earl of Aberdeen, Earl Grey and Robert Baden-Powell, then a Major-General and founder five years later of the Boy Scouts Association.

Booth certainly had a penchant for travelling and it will come as no surprise that after visiting the Holy Land and the Antipodes he should end up once again at the Royal Albert Hall, this time on 9th September 1905 and then only after a

Salvationists crowd the Royal Albert Hall for a dedication service in 1932.
B.B.C. Hulton Picture Library

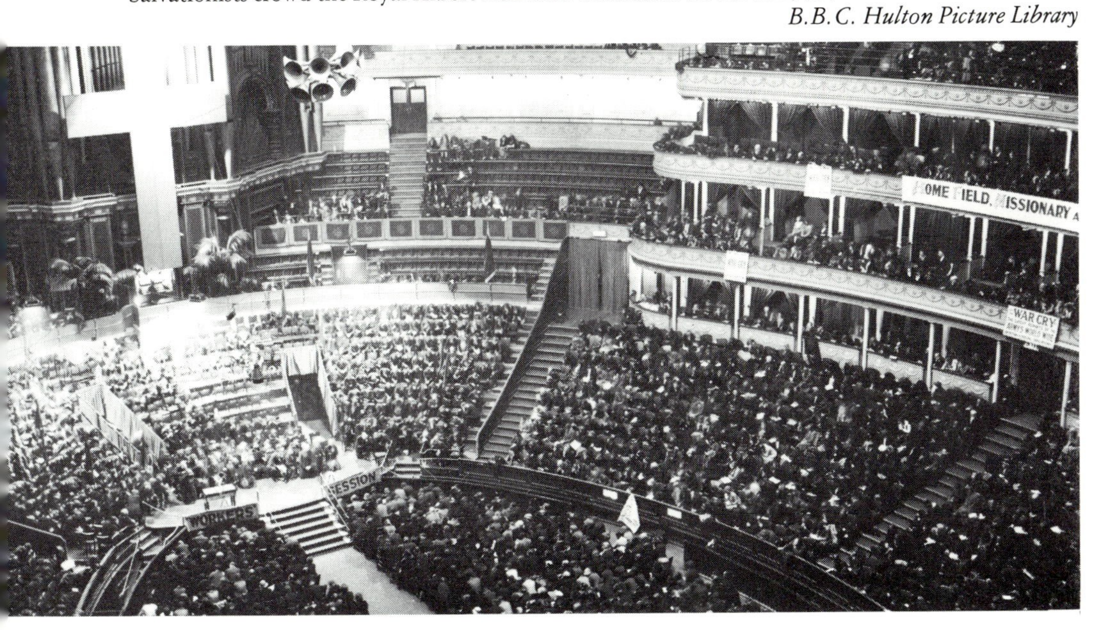

six weeks tour of England and Scotland which he commenced the day after he landed at Dover! The tour of the British Isles says much for the standards of the early days of motor engineering because it was carried out by Booth driving around in style in an A.C. car painted white and with red wheels. Now this show-piece was used to good effect when the cavalcade reached the Hall. Here there were the usual set pieces of bands playing, lusty singing and devotional prayers, with pictures of the General's travels thrown onto a large screen. After these somewhat protracted preliminaries, Booth's entourage appeared on the platform and then there was the profound silence of anticipation eventually broken by the sound of a car horn, the rubber bulb type of the early motoring days, and then the curtains, bearing a large portrait of the General, were drawn back to reveal the great man himself seated in his car. The faithful, having recovered from their leader's dramatic manifestation, were then regaled with a long account of his travels of the previous six months.

The Hall had not long to wait to before the Army paid its next visit. The 2nd October had been designated by the General a day of remembrance for all Salvationists who had died in the 40 years since the Army's foundation and gatherings were held in many parts of the world with Booth leading the prayer-ful thanksgiving in London. Once again the massed bands played and drew this remarkable tribute from George Bernard Shaw, who was certainly not the most charitable of critics:-

> "Massed Salvation Army Bands played the 'Dead March' from 'Saul' as I verily believe it has never been played in the world since Handel was alive to conduct it . . . "
>
> "I have heard Handel's great march snivelled through and droned through by expensive professional bands until the thought of death became intol-erable. The Salvationists, quite instinctively, and probably knowing . . . little of Handel, made it a magnificent paen of victory and glory that sent me—a seasoned musical critic of many years' standing—almost out of my senses with enthusiasm."

As if inspired by this unqualified praise it was decided to hold the first musical festival and it took place on 30th October 1907. There were drum and pipe bands and combinations for banjos and concertinas, chimes, handbells and tambourines all rounded off for good measure by the organ and a thousand strong choir. In his address the Army's Chief of Staff, Bramwell Booth, reflected and moralised on the inspirational effect that music can have on worship.

On 9th May 1912 General William Booth appeared for the last time in public and gave a moving peroration on what he had striven to achieve and his hopes for the future. It was his 83rd birthday and he was almost blind; many who were present probably sensed it was the last time they would see him. He died later the same year.

In the Summer of 1914 two meetings of the International Congress were held on 11th and 26th June but they were marred by a tragedy of the first magnitude as the Canadian contingent had been drowned on its way to Britain when the *Empress of Ireland* collided with a Norwegian freighter and sank in the St Lawrence. 130 Salvationists, including the Staff Band, perished and a memorial service was held in the Hall on 5th June led by General Bramwell Booth. Those lost were each represented by a chair draped with a white sash on which was a crimson cross and crown.

Another heart warming event occurred on 8th March 1926 when representatives from all over Europe gathered in the Hall to celebrate the 70th birthday of Bramwell Booth and 70 officers, one for each year of the General's life, dedicated themselves to a life of service on the other four continents. Just over three years later on 10th April 1929 the Prime Minister, Stanley Baldwin, presided over a celebration in connection with the centenary of the birth of William Booth. Government awareness of the great work done by this good man was reinforced by the appearance on the platform of many civic dignitaries and church leaders as well as the Army's new General, Edward J. Higgins. Bramwell Booth was the reason of the Salvation Army's first Royal occasion when the Duke and Duchess of York attended the Hall on 1st November 1934 to acknowledge the General's retirement. Not only did the future King George VI honour the gathering with his presence but he spoke also of the fine work done by the Army and its retiring leader.

In April, 1949 the Bandmasters' Council's Festival was held and the following month there was a Commissioning and Dedication of the Cadets of Peacemakers. Nearly 23 years after the Duchess of York's attendance she returned as Queen Elizabeth the Queen Mother to honour the Golden Jubilee Celebrations on 6th June 1957 of the National Home League, the women's organisation of the Army. Like her husband before her she praised the work of Salvationists, but in particular of the League on this special occasion. The William Booth Memorial Training College has held annual commissioning services during recent years and in 1964 produced a pageant entitled "Heroes of Faith". By then it was time for another Royal visit and on 24th June 1965 Queen Elizabeth II honoured with her presence the inaugural meeting of the Army's Centenary Celebrations at which the Archbishop of Canterbury, Arthur Michael Ramsay, the Cardinal Archbishop of Westminster, John Heenan, and the Home Secretary, Roy Jenkins, were also present on the platform with General Frederick Coutts. That year was a remarkable one for Army activity at the Hall, it being used on no less than fifteen occasions.

The World's Evangelical Alliance was addressed by Viscountess Davidson in 1946 and was probably the only organisation to celebrate Holy Communion in the Hall until, at the Eucharistic Congress on 3rd July 1958, High Mass was celebrated to mark the opening of the centenary year of the Church Union. An altar was erected in the Arena and covered with a white cloth on which six candles were placed. The thurifer with his censer, and servers, all in cassocks and surplices; the celebrant, deacon and sub-deacon in chasuble, tunicle and dalmatic of a shade deeper than gold. The ceremonial was elaborate, and carried out with dignity and precision; at the consecration six servers knelt in a row with candles complementing those on the altar. The congregation consisted of priests, sisters of religious orders, and laity, and there was a small choir of priests, next to the organ loft. That same month the Church of England Men's Society's National Rally was addressed by the Bishop and Provost designate of Coventry Cathedral and the Master of the Rolls, Lord Evershed.

The 300th Anniversary of the sailing of the Pilgrim Fathers was celebrated in 1921; and the 350th Anniversary on 23rd November 1970 with a pageant in four scenes illustrating freedom and faith—plea for freedom; searching for

The cross-bearer leads the procession out of the arena at the end of the service which forms part of the Festival of Remembrance.
C. Christodoulou

freedom; permissive freedom and disciplined freedom. The chairman was Admiral Sir Horace R. Law who introduced the United States Ambassador, Walter H. Annenberg, who in turn handed a message from President Nixon to Dr Billy Graham.

In May 1982 a Festival of Christ, an evening of word, music and drama with David Watson, received the united sponsorship of four famous London churches, All Souls, Langham Place; Holy Trinity, Brompton; St Helen's, Bishopsgate; and St Michael's, Chester Square.

All the diverse organisations mentioned so far have the common factor of promoting the Christian ethic and the morality and precepts stemming from Christ's teaching of the Word of God, so perhaps the last few words of this chapter might well be devoted to those of alien creeds.

On 27th January 1967 commemorative meetings were held in respect of the Guru Gubend Singh Tercentenary and in May, 1974 the Maharishi staged a World Plan Week during which there were lectures and seminars on such topics as business, education, government and health based on the precept "To solve the age-old problems of mankind in this generation". Prior to his appearance the holy man had insisted that the backstage area be scrubbed and there were also problems in preventing him from gazing on anyone of the female sex. The Maharishi paid another visit to the Hall in 1980.

The tercentenary of the Martyrdom of Bahadur was honoured on 3rd January 1976 by the Guru Teg Bahadur. On the same day the International Supreme Council of Sikhs organised a lecture and meetings were held on 9th April 1977 and 26th May 1979; on 29th January 1978 it celebrated the 400th Anniversary of Sri Amritsar, the speakers being Earl Mountbatten of Burma, Baron Brockway, Stanley Bidwell, Bernard Wetherhill, the Indian High Commissioner and various Sikh leaders.

Last but by no means least are the Bahaists who from 28th April—2nd May 1963 mounted what was probably the most colourful religious gathering ever seen in London. It was a World Congress to commemorate the centenary of the founding of their faith by Baha u'llah, a faith based on Babism and emphasising the value of all religions and the spiritual unity of all mankind. The Congress had the support of Dame Sybil Thorndyke and Dr Julian Huxley and was attended by delegates from most European countries as well as Ethiopians, Adenese, Iranians, Americans, Laotians, Indians, Bolivian Indians, Japanese, Somalis, Red Indians, Eskimos, Australian Aborigines, Pacific Islanders and even a Dyak ex-headhunter. Surely spiritual unity in practice and what better way to end this religious history of the Hall.

CHAPTER NINE

Politics

FOR THE first 20 years of the Hall's existence politics was ruled out of contention by the phraseology of the Charter excluding it by implication if not expressly in words. Nowadays politics might justifiably be classed as an aspect of science but it certainly was not so in the eyes of Charter interpreters a century ago. However, the Supplemental Charter of 1887 gave the Council the necessary loop-hole to permit political lettings though six more years were to pass before it was activated. Section 9 (A) of the Supplemental Charter simply stated "The Hall may, in addition to the objects in our said Charter, be appropriated to . . . . Public or private meetings of any body of persons", further adding in Section 10 (A) that "The Council may . . . . . let the Hall aforesaid for any of the purposes hereinbefore authorised" and in Section 10 (B) "Arrange with individual Members of the Corporation for the exchange, purchase, renting or temporary user of their boxes or seats".

These few words were to have far reaching consequences for future activities in the Hall and were to enable its doors to be opened to a much wider spectrum of undertakings than had been originally envisaged or permitted.

Following these relaxations the Council in 1893 resolved that it was "prepared to let the Hall for political meetings provided that there be no distinction of parties, and that such letting be on one of the ten excepted days under the Supplemental Charter; details to be left to the manager".

Surprisingly the relaxations did not lead to an immediate flurry of requests for political meetings to be held in the Hall and it was not until the turn of the century and the entry into a new reign that the parties came to the conclusion that the great building was as good a place as any, and better than most, in which to hold forth on issues of the day. The new reign also coincided with the election of a new President of the Council in the person of the Earl of Pembroke & Montgomery, who as Sidney Herbert had graced the House of Commons for many years; also the selection from 316 candidates of a new General Manager, Hilton Carter. The former's influence and the latter's liberal attitude and outlook did much to sway the political pendulum and, as an ever useful by-product, swell the Hall's income. However, everything was not completely free and easy and in 1907, when the Fabian Society applied for use of the Hall, the application was rejected. The Supplemental Charter had stated that the Council "may" let the Hall for public or private meetings; there was no compulsion about it and the Council could always fall back on the original Charter and the objectives and likes and dislikes of the founding fathers. The Fabians were considered to be in the dislike category and were, as it is recorded, "not entertained".

The following year saw a complete volte-face when the Independent Labour Party was granted the use of the Hall to welcome back Keir Hardie from a recent world tour; the reason was flimsy enough, even allowing for going round the world being a little more difficult to accomplish in Edwardian days than it is today, but the application was approved, resulting in a capacity crowd of 10,000 turning up to welcome their hero on 5th April 1908. Speakers included William Crooks, George Lansbury and that arch Fabian, George Bernard Shaw; the chairman was Ramsay MacDonald, destined to be in sixteen years the first Socialist Prime Minister of Britain, but then Chairman of the Independent Labour Party and Secretary of the Labour Party, surely a curious mixture of allegiances. When Hardie rose to speak he was regaled with *For He's a Jolly Good Fellow* by a cheering standing audience and then proceeded to range over a variety of topics from the colonies to alcohol. 4,000 tickets had been sold prior to the meeting and the free seats of the Gallery were occupied long before the meeting began, preceded outside in the street by the singing of the *Red Flag* and the *Marseillaise.* So fashionable Kensington witnessed the sights and sounds of revolution as it was to continue to do on and off for another ten years in the Suffragette campaign for votes for women.

Actually this campaign had got under way at the Hall three years before Keir Hardie returned from his travels, though he in fact did much to support the movement. On 16th April 1908 Herbert Henry Asquith's Liberal Government took office and wasted no time in arranging a meeting at which all the Cabinet was present. This was too good an opportunity to miss so far as the Suffragettes were concerned and very soon banners proclaiming the cause were being unfurled accompanied by shouts of "Votes for Women" which eventually were drowned by the massive sonorities of the organ, as the stewards busied themselves ejecting the disturbers of the peace.

The Tariff Reform League held a meeting in 1907 but the year really belonged to the Suffragette movement as the first meetings were held and became regular features at the Hall. One novelty for the period was the announcement of the results of a self-denial week held by groups all over the country as a fund raising exercise. At a mass meeting in the Hall the financial gains were recorded on a giant apparatus operated by the Socialist reformer, Frederick William Pethick-Lawrence, who was later to achieve eminence in the Upper House; this gimmick coupled with the monetary success of the campaign and the capacity attendance in the Hall led to it being used effectively in the future for mass rallies of the movement and its allies. These included the Women's Social and Political Union and the National Union of Suffrage

Societies, the latter on one occasion being successful in persuading David Lloyd George to address a meeting. All these activities in support of the feminine vote inevitably drew fire from the opposition and the Anti-Suffragette movement once was able to employ an impressive array of support in the shape of five dukes, fifteen earls, five viscounts, 44 baronets and thirteen M.P.s, to say nothing of seven members of the Cabinet and one heroic female.

Disturbances by the Sufragettes continued as a matter of course to occur whenever the opportunity arose and ingenious subterfuges were employed to infiltrate the Hall. A woman was sniffed out one night by the caretaker's dog from her hiding place in one of the organ pipes and as she had a portable microphone in her possession the speakers on the platform would have received quite a surprise had her mission succeeded. On another occasion a woman concealed herself under the platform after a concert and apparently stayed there all night until discovered in the morning of the following day. Incidents such as these prompted the Hall authorities to make thorough searches of all likely hiding places prior to sensitive meetings being held and this procedure proved successful in that such incidents died out. Not so the protests. Perhaps the most successful of these occurred in 1908 when Lloyd George addressed the Women's Liberal Federation on the controversial topic of Votes for Women. This meeting was a heaven-sent opportunity for the militants and, in view of the organising group and the subject matter of the address, they had no difficulty in gaining admission to the Hall. The Women's Social and Political Union secured the whole of the row in front of the platform and upon being seated all the women removed their hats and replaced them with white caps; then as proceedings were about to commence they all stood up, discarded their outer garments and revealed themselves in the dress of inmates of Holloway Prison. Up to that point the protest had been silent but as soon as Lloyd George commenced his speech a women in the Balcony began a speech of her own; as stewards approached to eject her she produced a whip from beneath her clothing and successfully held them at bay for some time before being thrown out. The incident provoked immediate uproar with furious cries of recrimination and abuse being hurled from one part of the Hall to another, interspersed with the chanting of the well known and worn clichés of the women's movements. Poor Lloyd George didn't stand a chance and his 20 minute speech took over a couple of hours to deliver.

Eventually the ''Votes for Women'' meetings became so disturbed and chaotic that in 1913 the Council decided to refuse requests for the use of the Hall for such purposes. Even the Royal Family was not immune from the controversy; on 28th February 1914 the King and Queen were present at a Railwaymen's Concert when, at the conclusion of an item by the orchestra, a woman in the Auditorium began a propaganda exercise which brought retaliatory abuse from sections of the audience before the organ was brought into use to drown the shouts as the woman was ignominiously ejected.

Women must have become something of an embarrassment to Carter because in December, 1908 there were disturbances at a Women's Liberal Federation Meeting and, whilst a Women's Socialist and Political Union Meeting apparently passed off quietly on 28th May 1910, in 1915 the Union once more got itself into bad odour to the extent that Carter decided to cancel a proposed meeting and refund the deposit. The First World War had by then been in progress over a year and the meeting was being held ostensibly "To demand the loyal and vigorous conduct of the war". Such a good intention was diminished considerably and, from Carter's viewpoint, conclusively by some words contained in a circular put out by the Union. The offending sentence asserted that "Neither the honour nor the interests of the nation are safe in the present hands, and that in particular the Prime Minister (Herbert Henry Asquith) and Sir Edward Grey (the Foreign Minister) are unfit for the great and responsible positions they hold". Such heresy when the nation was fighting for its very existence was quite out of the question but it may well be recalled that a later Prime Minister and Foreign Secretary in a subsequent war suffered much the same treatment and they had to go.

Going back in time some eight years to 18th April 1907, political mud slinging was put in the background for a while during a great gathering of Empire leaders at a banquet organised in their honour by the 1900 Club, a Tory organisation whose President was Arthur James Balfour and Chairman, the M.P. for Wigtown, a Lord of the Treasury and a biographer and novelist, Sir Herbert Maxwell. The Prime Ministers present were Arthur Deakin (Australia); Sir Wilfrid Laurier (Canada); Dr Leander Jameson (Cape Colony); Frederick Moor (Natal); Sir Robert Bond (Newfoundland); Sir Joseph Ward (New Zealand) and Louis Botha (Transvaal). Amongst others attending were Balfour and Andrew Bonar Law, past and future Prime Ministers of Great Britain; the Marquesses of Lansdowne, Londonderry and Zetland and the Earl of Onslow. Apart from good food, drink and conversation the assembly was regaled by an ode entitled *England's Welcome* written by the Poet Laureate, Alfred Austin, and set to music by Percy Pitt. The decorations matched the splendid occasion. The 16,000 square feet of flooring was covered by a single Union Jack, thought to be the largest ever made. The red, white and blue motif was repeated in the Boxes and Balcony and the upper walls displayed British and Colonial flags, and shields depicting the arms of the United Kingdom and the countries of the Empire. An Imperial Crown composed of flowers was hung over the Arena and garlands connected it to the flags and shields.

On 3rd November 1918 the Labour Party hired the Hall. J. H. Thomas was the principal speaker, *The Red Flag* was sung and a red banner instructing the workers of the world to unite was hung across the platform. This episode was followed by another eleven days later at which the Party launched its election campaign with a "Hands off Russia" slogan. The two together convinced Carter that enough was enough, so that a rally in support of the League of Nations, due to take place towards the end of the month, was cancelled and the deposit returned. Carter's explanation was that "In view of the demonstrations of a revolutionary character that took place at the meetings here on the 3rd and 14th inst., on the part of Mr Lansbury's supporters, I do not think that my Council will be justified in their own interests in allowing the meeting arranged

A contrast to the "Hands off Russia" meetings of sixty years earlier: Mr Geoffrey Rippon, Conservative M.P. for Hexham, at a "Solidarity with Poland" rally in 1982. *C. Christodoulou*

for the 23rd to take place in the Royal Albert Hall". This was not political prejudice on Carter's part but a shrewd assessment that, if such meetings were allowed to continue, sooner or later there would be a breach of the peace probably involving injury to some of those present and or damage to the fabric of the Hall.

However, Carter's decision quickly came unstuck when members of the Electrical Trades' Union threatened to cut off the supply on the 27th November at the time the Peace Ball was to be held. As a sign of their earnestness a gang of men appeared outside the Hall on the 23rd, cut off the mains supply and informed Carter that if he attempted to have it reconnected the supply to the whole of the capital would be disconnected. That afternoon a concert given by the Royal Choral Society was presented by gas-light after which the Government intervened and "recommended' to the Council that restrictions on Labour Party meetings should be withdrawn in order to avoid further trouble with the Union and possibly others as well if they also became incensed by the Council's actions. Many times Governments have capitulated to Union pressure and threats but usually they hold out longer than occurred in this case. So the Peace Ball was duly held without interruption and the Labour Party meeting went ahead as scheduled and to add insult to Carter's injury so great was the ticket demand that the Hall was hired the following night for an overflow meeting.

This all proved to be rather inconsequential compared with what took place in November 1920 when a joint meeting by the Communist Party and the Hands off Russia Committee was held in celebration of the third anniversary of the Russian Revolution. The chairman was Arthur Macmanus, a well known revolutionary, who proceeded to expound his creed and philosophy in no uncertain terms, much to the delight and satisfaction of his audience which had started the meeting by singing the *Internationale* and cheering Lenin and the Revolution. Macmanus soon brought things to the boil with such vitriolic rhetoric as "While we are not prepared—more shame on us—to emulate the Russians, we ought at least to see that our Government has something better to do than subsidise pirates and buccaneers" and much more in like vein. Another speaker came up with the pearl of wisdom that "The day is not far distant, I hope, when we will meet in the Albert Hall to bless the revolution. We are out to change the present Constitution and, if it is necessary to save bloodshed and atrocities, we will have to use the lamp-post and the walls. What would a few Churchills or Curzons on lamp-posts be compared with Amritsar or with Ireland?" As the latter was mentioned the audience rose and, with organ accompaniment, sang *Hymn of the Martyrs*. Then the name of the King came into the reckoning and was bandied about to the accompaniment of booing and hissing. It was this latter incident rather than what had gone before that apparently settled the issue so far as the Council was concerned and no contrary recommendation was forthcoming when the next proposed meeting organised by the Communist Party was refused on the grounds that "Mr Coates, the Tenant, did not comply with Clause 16 of his Contract, by allowing, or making no protest against, the hooting of the King's name, and the speech, which subsequent events have proved to be subversive of law and order".

In 1921 George Lansbury attempted to hire the Hall for a May Day rally organised by the euphemistically named The First of May Celebration Committee. The speakers listed were Margaret Bondfield, Ernest Bevin and the "bloody revolution" preacher of the previous November's meeting. Bondfield and Bevin were innocuous enough but the "preacher" was more than sufficient reason for the letting to be denied. A similar fate befell a proposed meeting on the Irish problem to be addressed by the somewhat unlikely figure of the Archbishop of Melbourne, Cardinal Mannix. Equally unlikely was the promoter of the meeting—the National Federation of General Workers, in the person of its General Secretary, James O'Grady, M.P.

In January 1924, Ramsay MacDonald became the first Labour Prime Minister and on the 8th of the month he attended a Victory Celebration accompanied by some of his leading lieutenants—Margaret Bondfield, Clynes, Lansbury, Morrison, Smithies and Thomas; this gathering of the comrades was regaled, not only by rousing speech making, but also by rousing music making in which all joined for exultant renderings of the *Marseillaise*, the *Comrades' Song of Hope*, *England Arise*, the *Red Flag* and the *Workers' March*. Later in the year yet another meeting on the victory theme was held; this time it was to welcome the successful General Election candidates under the banner of The Cause of Labour is the Hope of the World. Then at the end of the year the London Labour Party staged a great rally for the financial support of the *Daily Herald*, though the event must have had a bitter sweetness about it since MacDonald's short lived Government had been defeated in November. The celebration in 1948 of the paper's 10,000th issue was held in more auspicious circumstances since Labour was back in power, the Prime Minister, Clement Attlee, giving the address.

As the beginning of 1924 saw Labour celebrating its election victory so the end of the year witnessed the National Union of Conservative and Unionist Associations holding its election victory celebrations on the 4th December. Again the address was given by the Prime Minister, but this time it was Stanley Baldwin, with Lord Curzon proposing a congratulatory resolution which was seconded by Neville Chamberlain. Singing and organ solos brought further merriment to the occasion as they did in 1927 when the First of May Celebration Committee was more fortunate than it had been six years previously, even though one revolutionary had merely been substituted for another—Harry Pollitt instead of Macmanus. Hardly a bigger contrast could be imagined when just over two months later the National Citizens' Union put on a Patriotic Pageant to celebrate the "Rout of the Reds" with speeches by Lady Asquith and Commander Locker Lampson. In December, revolution was again on stage when there was an Amnesty Demonstration and 10th Anniversary of the Russian Revolution Celebration organised by International Class War Prisoners' Aid; Macmanus and Pollitt yielding pride of place to another personality of the far left, Joe Beckett. 1928 was barely six weeks old when, to coincide with the new Parliamentary session and the opening of the London County Council election campaign, the National and London Labour Parties mounted a great rally supported by the London Labour Choral Union.

Sixteen months later MacDonald was back at Downing Street and the faithful were soon demonstrating their elation and loyalty again; this time the gathering was addressed by Margaret Bondfield, Greenwood, Hamilton, Lansbury, Lee and Phillips. During the 1920s the Conservative Party does not seem to have patronised the Hall as much as its opponents although the Prime Minister, Baldwin, did address the Women's Unionist Organisation in 1927. However, it certainly rectified the balance in the following decade, starting on 4th April 1930 when the Primrose League was addressed by Baldwin, then Leader of the Opposition, in the presence of Walter Elliot, Lord and Lady Ebbisham and Lord Strathcona and Mount Royal. In May of the following year Baldwin was again the speaker at a mass meeting which apparently did not do much to assist his or the Conservative Party's cause, since in August MacDonald was confirmed in office at the General Election. A few weeks before that happened there was a great display of Party Unity on an issue still bedevilling the world today; MacDonald, Baldwin and Lloyd George shared the platform at a conference in "Support of World Disarmament"—one of the few issues that could tempt Socialists, Conservatives and Liberals to share the same platform.

In the Spring of 1935 the Central Women's Advisory Committee of the Conservative Association held a mass meeting and on 8th July 1936 the Party celebrated the centenary of the birth of Joseph Chamberlain. There was a meeting on 3rd December that year of what might be termed the rearmament lobby led by Churchill but supported by members of all parties, including other right wing Tories, the leader of the Liberal Party, Sir Archibald Sinclair, leaders of the League of Nations Peace Ballot and representatives of many trade unions, including Sir Walter Citrine. This, of course, was the period of exposure of the woeful situation Britain was in vis-à-vis military parity with the continental dictatorships and Churchill was the foremost protagonist of the country's rapid large-scale rearmament. In the following May Neville Chamberlain succeeded Baldwin as Prime Minister and amidst the darkening days leading up to the outbreak of war he rallied national support for his government with a demonstration at which he and Sir John Simon, Malcolm MacDonald, the son of Ramsay, and Viscount Astor of Hever spoke. Chamberlain spoke again in the Spring of 1938 at a mass meeting of the Union of Conservative and Unionist Associations and in April 1939 the Primrose League had a Grand Habitation Demonstration attended by Lord and Lady Ebbisham, the Grand Master, Sir Kingsley Wood, and the Vice Chancellor, Sir Reginald Bennett. The Chancellor of the Exchequer, Sir John Simon, was principal guest.

If it was communists and fellow-travellers that caused trouble during the late teens and early 1920s then it was the fascists that created problems in the 1930s. Coincidentally in 1919 Adolf Hitler founded the National Socialist German Workers' Party and Benito Mussolini the Fascia di combattimento and they and their followers caused trouble for the Council in the run-up to the

Munich Crisis and the Second World War. The British Union of Fascists booked the Hall in April and October 1934 and the meetings, in spite of certain fears, went off without the slightest trouble. Indeed, the Spring meeting was so circumspect and decorous that the well known Liberal, A. J. Cummings, was inspired to comment that it was ''About as much like the beginnings of a political and economic revolution as a sports festival at Wembley''. Sir Oswald Mosley addressed his followers for an hour. Future events were to contrast strongly with the tranquillity of that occasion and disabuse Cummings' ideas of calm and tranquillity. In March 1935 Sir Oswald again addressed his followers in the Hall, but this time only ticket holders were admitted and outside a large number of police was required to keep in check a noisy, vociferous mob. Events in Europe had made the Metropolitan Commissioner of Police, Viscount Trenchard, realise that fascist assemblies in London could lead to trouble and he had approached the Council with the request that hirers of the Hall for political purposes should be forced under the letting terms to inform the police so that any necessary precautions might be taken against possible riotous behaviour or worse. So it was that from this point onwards forewarned was to be forearmed.

The rapidly deteriorating international situation led to mounting anger with the British Union of Fascists, which aggravated affairs by its members strutting about in their para-military uniforms and giving the notorious fascist salute to add to the provocation. It came as no surprise then in March 1936 that two and a half thousand police massed around the Hall in an endeavour to maintain law and order; only those members of the public who could produce tickets for the rally were allowed within half a mile of the Hall, which was also the limit put upon traffic and public transport. In spite of this unprecedented show of force and the banning by the Home Secretary and Commissioner of Police of counter-demonstrations the police cordon was pressurised at various points by hundreds of people trying to break through to the Hall; fists flew, bottles were thrown and truncheons were used and there is little doubt that there would have been serious trouble if the police precautions had not been taken.

Troublemakers had, however, managed to infiltrate the Hall and there was skirmishing, shouting, jeering and the waving of anti-fascist banners before the stewards and police managed to eject the offenders and the martial tone of the meeting was able to continue; the razzmatazz included bugle calls and drum rolls as Mosley appeared on the platform picked out in spotlights and the playing of patriotic music on the organ accompanied by enthusiastic singing from those assembled. These events finally ended any future attempts by the Union to hire the Hall and the restriction applied also to the other extreme of the political spectrum because in February 1937 a Communist inspired meeting was rejected by the Council, possibly to demonstrate its impartiality but also as a matter of prudence considering the speakers were to have been Aneuran

Bevan, Stafford Cripps, Harold Laski, James Maxton, Harry Pollitt and George Strauss. All these tensions and upheavals caused the Council to reconsider its attitude to political meetings and in 1938 the British Union of Fascists and in 1948 the Communist Party were denied any further bookings, a ban still in existence today. Applications were, however, becoming more frequent. Ideas were put forward and rejected for one reason or another but after all the discussion was over the position was left more or less as it was and remains to this day, namely that each application should be judged on its merits and without bias, the only consideration being the maintenance of law and order and the best interests of the Hall. The Council's attitude did not, however, satisfy Ellen Wilkinson that discrimination still did not prevail and in the House of Commons she put down a question to the Home Secretary asking if he was "Aware that the owners of the Albert Hall have decided that the Hall is not to be let for political meetings except those in support of the Government, and whether in view of this discrimination he is prepared to introduce legislation making this great national meeting place national property, available without distinction to all political parties?" The Home Secretary's predictable answer was yes, he was aware, but no, he was not proposing legislation.

As the Spanish Civil War mounted in intensity with Germany and Italy supporting General Franco's Republican forces, King Victor Emmanuel III of Italy was proclaimed Emperor of Ethiopia; Germany reoccupied the Rhineland; the Rome-Berlin Axis was formed and the Munich Crisis was about to break, a spate of meetings urging peace at any price was denied a platform at the Hall on the grounds that the situation was too delicate and dangerous for the boat to be rocked by the League of Nations Union and such way-out organisations as the British Youth Peace Assembly and the Russia Today Society, or even by a gentleman named Captain Cuthbert Reavely who desired simply to hold a Peace Meeting. However, again wishing to demonstrate complete impartiality, the Council decided to go the whole way and ban all public meetings for the time being.

Came the Second World War and political controversy was stilled for the duration but the Hall did witness on one occasion a great gathering of politicians of both left and right. On 28th September 1943 the National Conference of Women comprising representatives of women's organisations from all over the country assembled to hear members of the Government urge them to ever greater war-efforts. On the platform was a large gathering of the political hierarchy—the Minister of Labour and National Service, Ernest Bevin (chairman), the Prime Minister, First Lord of the Treasury and Minister of Defence, Winston Churchill; the Foreign Secretary, Anthony Eden; the Lord President of the Council, Clement Attlee; the Minister of Aircraft Production, Sir Stafford Cripps; the President of the Board of Trade, Hugh Dalton; the Minister of Food, Lord Woolton; the Minister of Health, Ernest Brown, and his

Parliamentary Secretary, Florence Horsburgh. Altogether 32 members of the Government were present and it is hardly likely any of the ladies left the Hall in the slightest doubt about their value to the nation; many no doubt reflected that it had taken the tragedy of war to bring together on the same platform

The Albert Hall management has more than once found itself in conflict with the Electrical Trades Union, but here Mr Frank Chapple, its general secretary, is a speaker at a meeting in the Hall.
C. Christodoulou

those to whom only a few years previously the whole idea would have seemed quite outrageous.

Out of the wreckage of war was born the United Nations and its birth was celebrated in London by a meeting attended by Eleanor Roosevelt, widow of the United States President, Franklin Delano Roosevelt; first President of the new organisation, Paul Henri Spaak; Dame Megan Lloyd-George, David's daughter; and Sir Walter Citrine. The meeting was chaired by Field Marshal Sir Harold Alexander and the short act of remembrance and dedication was conducted by the Archbishop of Canterbury.

M. Spaak visited the Hall again on 21st July 1950 accompanied by Paul

Reynaud, Salvador de Madariaga, Sir Winston Churchill and Leader of the Liberal Party, Clement Davies; they were there to lend support to the concept of a United Europe. For many years the Liberal Party had been quiescent, really since the great days of Lloyd George, but it came to life briefly in 1947 when a big rally of its supporters was staged. The slogan on that occasion was "We can govern Great Britain". Eleven more years were to elapse before the Liberal Party again met in the Hall; this was in November 1958 and the rally was for the purpose of stimulating an increase of £30,000 annually in the Party's fund raising activities. Charged with the task of encouraging the faithful to greater efforts were Jo Grimond, Frank Byers and John Arlott. The next rally was on 21st March 1963 and was the culmination of a six months' recruiting campaign and three years later another meeting was held, but all, electorally at least, had little impact.

The Primrose League held meetings each year between 1951 and 1954, Churchill addressing the first and third. He also visited the Hall in 1954 when he was principal speaker at a National Union of Conservative and Unionist Associations meeting.

Two years later the Russian leaders, Bulganin and Khrushchev made a state visit to Britain which proved too much to bear for Malcolm Muggeridge, well known for his stance against Communism. He attempted to hire the Hall for a protest meeting but was refused due to the possibility of a serious and perhaps violent disturbance taking place; a further delicate issue was that the visitors were due to be received by the Queen and she was, as a holder of 20 seats, a member of the Corporation. The contretemps that might have ensued could not be countenanced under any circumstances. As it happened Muggeridge's meeting was held in Manchester and passed off without any trouble.

Shades of 1919 also reared themselves in 1954 during the unofficial strike of members of the Electrical Trades' Union, which applied to use the Hall for a meeting on 22nd January and was refused because the dispute was not official. This rebuff lead to a threat to black-out the Hall and, worse still, to "black" it after the settlement of the dispute. Pickets were drafted and the Secretary of the Labour Party, Morgan Phillips, joined the lines as a sign of solidarity. The Council, foreseeing the possibility of such action developing, installed emergency lighting and employed non-union labour for its operation.

On 22nd May 1958 the Prime Minister, Harold Macmillan, supported on the platform by Sir Winston Churchill, Sir Anthony Eden and Lord Hailsham and other members of the Cabinet, addressed the Annual Conservative Women's Conference which he did again in May 1963, and Sir Alec Douglas-Home did in June of the following year.

The first public meeting of the Anti-Violence League, a non-party, non-sectarian organisation, took place on 28th June 1961 "to provide a specific channel through which public dissatisfaction with the state of the criminal law, with particular emphasis on crimes of violence, can be forcibly directly at Parliament''.

The National Union of Teachers held a rally on 20th November 1961, 2,000 members having to listen to the proceedings relayed outside due to the Hall being full; the teachers were in the midst of a pay dispute with the Minister of Education, Sir David Eccles. On 29th May 1962 there was a commendable showing of unanamity of viewpoint between certain members of the main parties even though it was only for an hour or two. Dame Irene Ward (Conservative) and Kenneth Robinson (Labour) were amongst the speakers at a rally of 7,000 nurses organised by the Staff Side of the Nurses and Midwives Whitley Council under the chairmanship of Jo Grimond (Liberal). Many M.P.s from all sides of the House were present to give support to the nurses as they discussed their profession's salaries claims and protested at the 6d (2½p) per hour increase offered by the Government.

Union agitation was again to the fore on 12th January 1971, when the T.U.C. organised a meeting to protest against the Industrial Relations Bill. Its General Secretary, Victor Feather, and the Leader of the Opposition, Harold Wilson, were given a hot reception; as they attempted to address the meeting they were booed and heckled because of their alleged lack of support for the power workers who had come out on strike against the Bill. This sort of political pressure manifested itself again on 20th March 1976 when a campaign meeting was organised by the ''Fight for the Right to Work'' movement.

The Second World War seems to have been the watershed so far as mass political meetings are concerned. Before they were commonplace; since they have dwindled to insignificant proportions, are widely spaced and are frequently concerned with either industrial affairs or have foreign overtones.

In 1953 the Menorah Fund Committee met to publicise Britain's gift to the newly founded state of Israel—a large menorah* which now stands close to the Knesset precincts in Jerusalem. The 10th anniversary of the state was celebrated in April, 1958; the speakers included Dame Megan Lloyd George and Earl Balfour, nephew of Arthur James Balfour, architect of the Balfour Declaration of 1917 which pronounced British support for the establishment of a national home for the Jews in Palestine; a national home that also celebrated its 20th anniversary in the Hall in 1968.

One hundred and twenty stewards were on duty on 8th April 1959 when a meeting called by the Labour Party to protest over the situation in Central Africa and Nyasaland was held. As things turned out their presence was a wise precaution since trouble soon arose. It was signalled by the discharge of a firework under one of the seats when the Chairman of Christian Action, Canon John Collins, was speaking. Leaflets urging the prohibition of further coloured

*A seven branched candelabrum used in ceremonies.

and foreign immigration into Great Britain were then thrown and there were shouts of "Keep Britain White" before 14 of the trouble makers were ejected by the stewards after a struggle. The disturbance was the work of the National Labour Party, a breakaway group from Sir Oswald Mosley's Union Movement. The Shadow Colonial Secretary, James Callaghan, the President-General of the Southern Rhodesian African National Congress, Joshua Nkomo, and the Rev Michael Scott were the other speakers.

In 1964, the Prime Minister of India, Jawaharlal Nehru, one of the country's founding fathers, died and shortly afterwards a Memorial Meeting was attended by the Prime Minister, Sir Alec Douglas-Home, the Leader of the Opposition, Harold Wilson, Lord Attlee, Macmillan, Arnold Toynbee and Kingsley Martin. The Foreign Affairs Circle organised a meeting in 1967 under the chairmanship of Lord St Oswald; it had the title "Britain Remembers the Victims of Communism", victims not only from within the Soviet Union but also those who had escaped from fascist tyranny only to fall into the malevolent power of an equally evil regime. This sort of thing had cast its shadow nearly 10 years earlier when the *Daily Worker* had organised a rally for the purpose of applying pressure for the closure of United States bases in England and the stopping of H-bomb patrols, thereby doing away with the cornerstone of Britain's deterrent against that self-same despotism. The following year, 1959, this newspaper celebrated its 24th birthday with a rally addressed by that remarkable prelate and apostle of the left, the "Red" Dean of Canterbury, Dr Hewlett Johnson. As if to level the balance between left and right the Greek Committee Against Dictatorship held meetings on 26th April and 28th June 1970 protesting against the excesses perpetrated by the fascist regime of the Colonels, then darkening the face of that ancient civilisation.

The political scene in the Hall to date quietly drew to a close in a rather unconventional manner with the Peace Pledge Union putting on a concert in October 1973 and the Indian High Commission holding a meeting on 12th June 1977. So the Hall's political commitment has for all practical purposes gone full circle, at least for the time being. From the days when the Charter forbade the subject to be discussed or propagated to the days when parties and groups are no longer interested in espousing their causes under the great dome; from the days when people and parties would have liked to have used the Hall for political debate and demonstration but were debarred and would have been welcome for financial reasons if nothing else, to the days when permissively and economically they would be welcome but are themselves totally disinterested.

CHAPTER TEN

The Charitable and Commercial Business

CHARITIES have already been touched upon in earlier chapters, but there are many more which are equally deserving of attention since in spite of all the panoply of the welfare state public finance falls far short of meeting all the requirements for the country's wellbeing and, of course, there are a large number of causes which do not have the good fortune to come under the state's umbrella at all.

Wars and natural disasters are occurrences which make an immediate impact and regrettably they are all too frequently with us. In the former category we can go back to obscure conflicts of long ago; to 1879 and the incident at Isandlwana in Zululand, where a body of British troops was almost annihilated by an overwhelming Zulu force, only 40 of the soldiers out of a total of 800 escaping. Also in the same year to one of today's trouble spots, Afghanistan, where troops under General Roberts gained a brilliant victory at Kandahar resulting in Abdur Rahman, a ruler favourable to British interests, being placed upon the throne. These incidents resulted in charities being instigated on behalf of both cases—the Isandlwana Fund and the Afghan War Relief Fund. They benefited respectively in 1880 and 1881 by what were termed ''military assaults-at-arm'' but were in fact displays in which Aldershot Gymnasium staff was joined by Army and Naval personnel in something resembling a cross between a tattoo and the Royal Tournament. The first display raised £500 and was attended by the Prince and Princess of Wales and the Commander-in-Chief, the Duke of Cumberland. The Royal couple were present again the following year at an even more glittering performance; the Band of the 1st and 2nd Life Guards, and the Grenadier, Coldstream and Scots Guards provided the music and a good deal of the spectacle. Demonstrations of fencing, bayonet and lance fighting, sword play, boxing and wrestling were coupled with Scottish dancing and a gymnastic display by the Highland Light Infantry, the Gordon Highlanders, the London Scottish Volunteers and H.M.S. *Excellent* with substantial support by 300 representatives from the German Gymnastic Society. To round off the performance a detachment of the Royal Horse Artillery stripped down a 9-pounder gun and put it together again in something like two and a half minutes. Under what circumstances the boxing and wrestling were permitted is unclear but it may have been something to do with them benefiting war charities that overcame the Prince's repugnance of pugilism and the inhibitions imposed by the Charter.

Both World Wars were still further reasons for charitable effort and the public was not found wanting. Concerts were popular methods of raising money and several of these are referred to in the chapter on music, but other means were not discounted. In December, 1917 a Tombola and Petticoat Lane Fair was held in support of Miss Lena Ashwell's Concerts at the Front; on 8th November 1918 a Grand Concert by the Beecham Symphony Orchestra, with popular songs thrown in for good measure, was in aid of the King's Fund; on 18th December 1919 in the presence of the King and Queen the Massed Bands of the Brigade of Guards joined forces with Melba, Clara Butt, Tom Burke and Kennerley Rumford for the benefit of the Guards' Home for Daughters of Guardsmen. On 2nd August 1942 the London Fire Service Benevolent Fund was the recipient of the proceeds from a Grand Celebrity Concert in which some of the most popular stars of music and variety appeared: there were Mantovani and his Orchestra; Troise and his Mandoliers; Lev Pouishnoff; Joan Hammond and Dennis Noble from the world of music and the variety stage was represented by Lupino Lane; Stanley Holloway; Douglas Byng; Harold Fielding; Max Miller; G. S. Melvin; Vera Lynn; Elsie and Doris Waters; and Nervo and Knox.

One of the most successful events ever held occurred shortly after the Supplemental Charter of 1887 gave the Council power to exclude seatholders from events in the Hall which was let for £500 for the Centenary Festival of the Masonic Institution for Girls. It was attended by the Institution's President, the Prince of Wales, accompanied by the guest of honour, the King of Denmark. 1,400 supporters witnessed a display in the Arena and then sat down to a banquet laid on tables placed round the Amphitheatre in a series of ellipses the full circuit of the Hall. The rest of the building was packed with specially invited guests and the incredible sum of £51,000 was raised. The Theatre was in use for a concert in 1888, for the benefit of Princess Frederica's Convalescent Home. The following year an Ice Carnival, Bazaar and Festival was mounted during the second week of February. The Carnival took place in the Theatre, the necessary freezing arrangements no doubt being accomplished by the newly emergent power of electricity; the Bazaar and Festival were accommodated in the Hall and the Horticultural Society's Conservatory and the whole affair was promoted by William Whiteley, a Yorkshireman, who pioneered the department store in London and whose business still flourishes in the capital today. The hiring charge of the Theatre was £40 and that for the Hall £300, inclusive of staffing, lighting and police; cheap at the price considering a profit of £3,150 was made and donated to the West London Hospital.

Children came into the reckoning in 1913 when the newspaper *Truth* used the Arena for a toy and doll show prior to distributing the exhibits and proceeds to hospital and workhouse charities in London at Christmas. On 3rd January 1919 Princess Patricia of Connaught gave her patronage to a matinée performance in aid of the Invalid Children's Aid Association, which had the

A bazaar in aid of the Charing Cross Hospital held in the Royal Albert Hall in 1899.
Royal Albert Hall

support of Princess Mary on 30th November 1971; it also benefited in 1973 from a concert given in the presence of Princess Margaret by Up with People, a popular song and dance company, and Arthur Howes and Eddie Jarrett.

From 21-24th May 1930 the British Legion organised a British Empire Service League Empire Fair with such things as books, china, glass and "white elephant" stalls. Even more ambitious was the King of Glory Pageant promoted by the Oxford House Settlement; an outstanding event one supposes since it lasted from 15-27th February 1937 and had the support of the Fairbairn (of *Hiawatha* fame) Pageant Choir. Between the Wars the Barnardo Young Helpers' League sometimes hired the Hall for fund raising purposes; and there were the happy occasions on 28th September 1935 and 21st August 1937 when respectively the Hall was used for a children's celebration of George V's Silver

Jubilee, and a tea party and entertainment for Westminster schoolchildren to celebrate George VI's Coronation.

The Royal Watermen's Almshouses, Penge, benefited from a Variety Fair on 10th October 1952; there was a star studded cast of Julie Andrews, Charlie Chester, Robert Easton, Alfred Marks, Anne Shelton and Elsie and Doris Waters with Leslie Roberts' Twelve Television Toppers, Peter Yorke and his Concert Orchestra and the Ford Motorworks Military Band. The United Appeal for the Blind was helped by the presence of the Duchess of Kent on 4th December 1953 and Princess Alice and the Duke of Athlone supported the Music for Charity Society on 24th October 1954. The National Spastics Society put on a Children's All Nations Calvalcade of Song and Dance directed by Rus Hardy in 1956 and it also promoted a performance of William Walton's *Belshazzar's Feast* on 6th June 1979. The Friends of Jewish Agricultural Training had money raising efforts in 1958/9 and again in 1970 when the function incorporated International Ballroom Championships; and the Pestalozzi Village was the recipient of the proceeds of a Scottish Swiss Festival organised in 1959 by the Payling Music Society. Princess Margaret was present at the Dr Barnardo's Homes event on 22nd October 1966 and the National Children's Home was honoured by the presence of the Duchess of Gloucester on 12th April 1969 when it celebrated its centenary. This was certainly a jolly, happy affair which included a historical survey of the Home's first hundred years—the *Story of a Family*—and the B.B.C. birdman, Percy Edwards; Bob Arnold of the B.B.C.'s long running serial *The Archers*; Cyril Jackson's one man band; and Johnny Morris. Also the children gave displays of agility gymnastics and five-a-side football.

The London Wexfordmen's Association organised a Kennedy Brothers Memorial Concert on 22nd November 1970. There was a big array of Irish performers taking part to raise funds for a centre for Wexford emigrants in London and to honour the Kennedys' name.

The Cinema and Television Benevolent Fund stages an annual "Filmharmonic", each designated by the year in which it is produced. As the name implies, film music is the cornerstone and in 1970, when the initial event was held, the R.P.O. was conduced by Elmer Bernstein, Ron Goodwin, Henry Mancini and Muir Mathieson in a programme of nostalgia from old and new films, including James Mason in the narrator's role in excerpts from Shakespeare's *Henry V* the music for which film was by William Walton. For the 1973 Festival the compere was Michael Parkinson and the music provided by Geoff Love and his Orchestra featuring compositions by Legrand and Nino Rota. That also was the year when a Festival was held by the National Society for Mentally Handicapped Children; and the N.S.P.C.C. was indebted to Dionne Warwick for the concert on 22nd February 1975. That same year the Royal Marines Band and Roger Whittaker in concert participated in a gala evening on

1st October in aid of life saving and organised jointly by the Royal National Lifeboat Institution, the St John Ambulance Association, the Peter Fry Rescue Trust and the Royal Life Saving Society; one of the attractions was a fashion show presented by Marks & Spencer Limited. Also in 1975 Lions International had a private function and then on 28th October 1976 and 20th October 1977 the British Polio Fellowship was favoured by the Elsa Wells International Ballroom and Latin-American Dance Championships.

"Start Christmas with Richard Baker" was the title of a concert on behalf of John Groom's Association for the Disabled on 21st December 1976. The Royal Marines Orchestra and Goldsmiths Choral Union with organist, Anne Marsden Thomas, and baritone, John Lawrenson, participated in Christmas music and carols, and there was more work for the orchestra in Offenbach's Overture *La Belle Hélène* and excerpts from Delibes' ballet *Sylvia*, and from the Choir in Handel's *Zadok the Priest.* The year after there were a couple of concerts in aid of the Migraine Trust and the Association for Spina Bifida and Hydrocephalus. The Multiple Sclerosis Fund and the Musician's Benevolent Fund were happy to join in the 65th birthday celebrations on 15th April of a Devonshire mechanic, Ron Davy, who had run a youth orchestra for 30 years in Tiverton and had always dreamed of playing in the Royal Albert Hall. Now he did just that, paying £950 in rental and bringing along with him a 190 member orchestra, which included some old boys and girls.

So much for the charitable business; what of the commercial business? Well, this can and does take several guises like promotional exhibitions, shows, demonstrations and even sporting events. Many examples of these recall the Inaugural Mass Meeting of the Trade Defence Union in 1931 and the National Nylon and Industrial Textile Trade Fairs staged respectively in March and April, 1958. These were followed by the International Watch and Jewellery Fair and Exhibition held from 26-30 September when approximately 150 firms exhibited their wares in the Boxes at a fee of between £50-£150 for the week, inclusive of stands. The following November, Miss World, Penelope Coelen of Durban, modelled swim suits at an International Fashion Fair. The same month there was an Empire Rally in support of Commonwealth Trade organised by the Commonwealth and Empire Industries Association. Lord Balfour of Inchrye was in the chair and the Prime Minister, Harold Macmillan, and the Leader of the Opposition, Hugh Gaitskell, were present to listen to the speeches, one of which was made by the Prime Minister of Canada, John Diefenbaker.

The International Dairy Congress was the first to be held in London for 31 years when it was opened by the Queen Mother on 29th June 1959. The British Opthalmic Trade Fair was the setting for a display of British opthalmic optical products from 4-7th July 1961. The World Congress of Man Made Fibres was the scene from 1-4th May 1962 of what must be classed as the most lavish and expensive of all business activities ever held in the Hall and must be near the

Queen Elizabeth the Queen Mother arriving at the Royal Albert Hall for a University of London presentation of degrees ceremony. *Lauri Tjurin*

top of the list of any other form of activity as well. The Congress had been opened by the Queen Mother and was attended by 3,000 delegates from 40 countries, the Secretary of State for the Colonies, Reginald Maudling, other government ministers, ambassadors and representatives of industry. The entertainment, called a ''Soirée de Gala'', produced by Franco Zeffirelli, who was also the Artistic Director, at an estimated cost of £75,000 was presented by 1,000 performers for 5,000 guests. The Philharmonia Orchestra was conducted by Sir Malcolm Sargent and there were the Pipers of the Black Watch and choirs and dancers brought specially from all over the world. The stars included Victoria de los Angeles, Guiseppe di Stefano, Yehudi Menuhin, Pilar Lopez, Jean Babilee, Elsa Marianne von Rosen, Anna Russell and the Peters Sisters, and the programme ranged from a May Day Carnival, which transformed the Arena into a whirling mass of colour, to Verdi's *Hymn to the Nations*. The whole arrangement was set against the opulence of Zeffirelli's décor and was rounded off by a ball and supper.

Attracting the customer has been practised in the Hall for well over a century and probably the most fascinating of all the enterprises that have used it was the first to do so. From 1876-87 Scotts' Sewage Company rented accommodation and plied its trade, although it is not clear exactly how or in what form it operated. Suffice to say that Henry Cole recorded that one day on a visit he had found a certain Gilbert Redgrave at work in his office "getting ammonia from urine".

In 1904 there was a Chemical Exhibition followed 10 years later by a *Daily Mirror* Dress Matinée at which the Shadow Corset Company displayed chemises at 6/6d (32½p) each and nightgowns at 10/6d (52½p) each. *The Sphere* did something similar, although probably in a more sophisticated manner, in 1946 when it promoted a Midnight Dress Show given by 22 fashion houses employing 150 mannequins. 1931 was the year the motor car first entered the Hall when on 27th April a new Hillman model was launched on the market, the vehicles being exhibited in the Arena and a luncheon given for trade representatives. The Ford Motor Co. was even more ambitious five years later when its models were on show for 10 days. In February and March 1972 British Rail joined forces with the R.P.O. and the composer, pianist and educator, Antony Hopkins, to present a couple of musical teach-ins, admission being by combined train and concert ticket.

Whitesquare (U.K.) Limited put on hairdressing displays in 1975 and 1976 as did Grand Metropolitan Hotels Limited in the three years commencing 1978. The major event of this kind, however, is the annual competition for the L'Oréal Colour Hairstyle Trophy donated by Golden Limited.

The World Hairdressing Congress was held over two days in 1982. The first day was concerned with the World Top Hairstyling Award and the British and French 1980 World Championship Team, while the second day was devoted to Remy International, Marlies Moller, Masa Ohtake and the winner of the World Top Hairstyling Award, Gigi Gandini.

With the world recession biting deeply into Britain's trade, the Institute of Sales and Marketing Management chose the Hall as the venue for what was described as "Britain's first national multi-industry sales convention" in June 1983. The speakers booked for the convention included John Fenton, founder and chief executive of the Institute of Sales and Marketing Management, who has been called "the Billy Graham of Selling," and the programme included a session entitled "How to get customers banging on your door and begging for more".

The Institute of Directors and its Annual Conference is probably the best known and well publicised business gathering of the year. The Institute has a membership of about 30,000 and devotes its energies to representing the interests of company directors and encouraging their professional competence. Usually about ten per cent of the membership attends each conference and the proceedings have developed more or less into a set pattern from year to year with the organ being played pianissimo as the assembly gathers to hear the President's opening address and the speeches by eminent academics, businessmen and women, politicians and, occasionally, members of the Royal Family. In 1961 the directors were addressed by two Prime Ministers, Harold Macmillan, and Sir Roy Welensky of the Federation of Rhodesia and Nyasaland. The Duke of Edinburgh was present in 1962 and 1980 and took the opportunity of enlisting industrial support for his Award Scheme. In 1970 the Prince of Wales was one of the speakers as was Prince Bernhard of the Netherlands in 1973. On the former occasion the other speakers were the

The layout for a commercial banquet in the Royal Albert Hall. *Royal Albert Hall*

EXIT
EXIT
EXIT

Chairman of Courtaulds Limited, Lord Kearton; the General Secretary of the T.U.C., Victor Feather, and the Mayor of New York, John Lindsay. On the latter occasion they were the Prime Minister, Edward Heath, the Chairman of the British Aircraft Corporation, Sir George Edwardes, the Countess of Dartmouth, the former United States Treasury Secretary, John Connally, and the Metropolitan Anthony of Sourozh. The 1974 meeting was memorable for the heated argument on the subject of strikes between the Chairman of Vickers Limited, Lord Robens, and the General Secretary of the T.U.C., Len Murray, in presence of Margaret Thatcher, who became leader of the Conservative Party the following year.

The setting of these august meetings is somewhat theatrical in that the platform is illuminated by floodlights with the rest of the Hall in virtual darkness and there is a large television screen installed above the organ so that a closed circuit picture of the speakers can be seen by the audience, not always an easy thing to do in the flesh due to the magnitude of the Hall. The screen also serves as a display board for the Institute's services and as a call medium for anyone who might have been found missing from his office desk. During coffee and lunch breaks and in the pauses between speeches it is also used for keeping the company aware of city news and stockmarket information. As the show costs a sum in the region of £25 per head it is important that one should receive a good lunch as some recompense and this is served up in individual boxes containing such delicacies as pâté, cold meats, salad and a bottle of wine and eaten by the members where they are seated to the sound once more of the organ.

In 1980 the Institute of Directors was challenged for the title of most prestigious business event of the year when Lloyd's of London hired the Hall for the first time on 4th November to discuss changes in its constitution.

It is a far cry from Scotts' Sewage Company to the Institute of Directors and Lloyd's of London but they and all the other business houses and associations that periodically have used the Hall for their various activities have added a dimension that few perhaps connect with the great building. When charitable operations are additionally taken into account the dimension becomes very large indeed and bears comparison with most of the other pursuits that go on within.

The annual conference of the Institute of Directors, with Institute members eating their lunch out of individual boxes served to them in their seats. *Institute of Directors*

CHAPTER ELEVEN

Sport

MANY sports are, by their very nature, impossible to stage in the Hall but within its limitations most make an appearance from time to time; some have been and gone for various reasons but others came and have remained in varying degrees of regularity. Even those that cannot be practised have had connections such as the meetings of the Metropolitan Police Athletics Association, and the Lords Taverners' dinner on 21st October 1958 when presumably there was plenty of cricket talk and reminiscence.

There is little doubt that the most unusual event was also amongst the very first to take place and is the one and only time that an athletic track has been laid. The occasion was a race of the Marathon distance of 26 miles 385 yards, or 520 times round a coconut matting surfaced circuit of some 90 yards, between C. W. Gardiner and Dorando Pietri. The date was 18th December 1909 and the result was something of an anti-climax since Pietri retired during the 482nd lap, ostensibly because of problems created by the new shoes he was wearing; Gardiner carried on for the full distance and so won a race that never was.

If the contest between Gardiner and Pietri was the most unusual then that for the Wightman Cup in November 1978 must rank as the most absorbing and dramatic. Tennis was a comparatively new introduction only having made its initial appearance eight years previously, but this match, the 50th between the ladies of Great Britain and the United States, more than made up for anything the Hall might have missed in its first hundred years. The destination of the Cup depended on the outcome of the final confrontation; this was between Virginia Wade and Sue Barker and Chris Evert and Pam Shriver; the British pair being triumphant in a close three set match. So ended a memorable nail-biting cliff-hanger contest with pandemonium reigning in the Hall as Virginia and Sue hugged each other and the whole team covered in Union Jacks were pelted with flowers by spectators beside themselves with excitement and the relief of almost unbearable tension. Millions of others rejoiced in their own homes—in front of television sets.

Alas, this great British victory was not destined to be repeated two years later when the United States retained the Cup it had won back in America in the intervening year. This time, with the Duke and Duchess of Kent amongst the spectators, the United States was triumphant by five matches to two but the result could so easily have been as narrow as it was in 1978 though this time with the Americans clinching matters in the last match. That this was so was due to the astonishing collapse of the British captain, Virginia Wade. In a match which was described as one of the most astonishing in the Cup's history and possibly also in the whole history of tennis, Chris Lloyd beat her 7-5, 3-6, 7-5 "in an escape which made Houdini seem like a novice". Virginia led 5-1 and 40-15 in the final set and yet not only squandered the two match points but proceeded to lose the next six games as well, much to her distress and mortification. Pundits will argue for years how such a dramatic turn round of fortune could happen but happen it did and ensured the Cup remaining on the other side of the Atlantic for another year. In 1982 the British girls were again heavily defeated by their American opponents.

The Wightman Cup matches were sponsored by the Carnation Foods Co., in conjunction with the Lawn Tennis Association and it was sponsorship by the tobacco firm, Rothmans Limited, that first brought the game to the Hall in March, 1970. There was much discussion about the playing surface before the decision was made to utilise the old dance floor; the boards were found to be uneven and had to be covered with "Nyegrass", a fibre carpet, to make the court playable. On New Year's Day, 1970, Christine Janes and Joyce Williams followed by Jaroslav Drobny and David Lloyd played exhibition matches to test the court's suitability for top class players and so became the first of the many that were to follow.

In the first year Rothmans had hit on the idea of offering the Grand Tier Boxes to companies and individuals complete with food and drink so that they could entertain their customers and friends in style, preferably in evening dress. The innovation proved popular and was retained by public demand in future years.

Rothmans, however, soon got a rival in tennis promotion at the Hall. In 1970 the whisky firm of John Dewar & Sons staged the final of the Dewar Cup, a tournament that became in the third year part of the International Lawn Tennis Federation's Commercial Union Grand Prix, inaugurated in 1968. The preliminary rounds were played in different parts of the country with the finals providing yet another big occasion at the Hall. Singles and doubles were played but, unlike Rothmans International the Dewar Cup brought the ladies into battle also, the ladies' events being part of the Colgate International series. Dewar's decision to become part of the Grand Prix circuit, in which players compete for points as well as prize-money as they tour the world, meant that the standard of play was raised to higher levels because the entry included most of the world's top players. A novel feature of the Dewar Cup finals was that the contestants were preceded onto court by a piper and the spectators entertained by the British Caledonian Airways Pipe Band in full Highland dress.

Both firms have now ceased their sponsorship at the Hall but Mazda Cars Limited sponsored a tournament in 1979 for players over 35, which certainly provided plenty of nostalgia for the older buffs. This event, called the G. B. Classic, featured players such as Mark Cox, Cliff Drysdale, Neil Fraser, Pancho Gonzales, Rex Hartwig, Bob Hewitt, Frew McMillan, John Newcombe, Tom Okker, Alex Olmedo, Ken Rosewall, Frank Sedgman, Fred Stolle and Roger Taylor. As Lew Hoad was the referee the connoisseurs were well provided with material for reminiscence. In January 1983 the Barrett World Doubles Tennis Championship was held for the first time at the Hall. It was won by the Swiss-Hungarian combination of Heinz Guthardt and Balasz Taroczy, who defeated

An international badminton match between England and the People's Republic of China in 1981.
C. Christodoulou

the American-Mexican pair Brian Gottfried and Raoul Ramirez in the final 6-3, 7-5, 7-6.

Table tennis came to the Hall between the wars and the World Championships were staged in 1938 as were the English Championships a year later and in 1960. The *Daily Mirror* promoted a national tournament in 1954 and there was an international event six years later with the European Championships being played in 1971. In 1973 the finals of a Royal Albert Hall sponsored tournament took place in the Hall on 3rd February. The money raised went towards the £45,000 needed to provide facilities for the disabled at the Hall, including ramps and a special lift, and each player was sponsored to the extent of a penny per point. This was the first tournament of its kind ever organised on such a scale with preliminary rounds being played in each of the capital's boroughs with the mayors giving their patronage; and at stake from the players' point of view, apart from the satisfaction of helping a worthwhile cause, was the possibility of winning one of the four cups put up for competition.

It is surprising that it was not until 1979 that badminton was played at the Hall but an excellent start was made, the Friends' Provident Life Office sponsoring the first ever World Open Tournament which brought most of the game's greatest players to London. The company was responsible also for promoting an international match between England and the People's Republic of China on 4th May 1981. Just twelve months later the men's world team badminton championship for the Thomas Cup was held in the Hall in the presence of Her Majesty the Queen.

Basketball championships have been held but were not crowd pullers and have lapsed in recent years; on 28th February 1969 a team from English schools played against children from United States bases in Britain but that is as far as internationalism has gone, although during the Second World War the United States Army held a few championships.

Five-a-side football has been played, the *Daily Express* promoting a tournament in 1969 but, like basketball, it has not proved popular in the Hall.

During the 1960s and 1970s gymnastics really took off as a spectator sport thanks largely to the superlative accomplishments of Eastern European and Japanese exponents whose prowess was brought to the notice of the British public by means of television. On 17th October 1970 Britain competed against the United States but the first international event of major consequence is still awaited when the stars from the East would be expected to compete. The British Amateur Gymnastic Association holds a championship meeting each year at which the best performers in the country make their contributions. The *Daily Mirror* has also promoted a National Gymnastics tournament and on 17th January 1981 the Girls' Championships were staged. Competition at these levels is helping to raise standards so that hopefully in a few years British gymnasts will be able seriously to challenge for supremacy at the top level. In spite of Britain

not being up to world standards the first and second World Open Trampoline Championships were held in the Hall on 21st March 1964 and 30th January 1965 respectively.

Keeping fit is certainly a priority requirement in the making of a successful gymnast and the Keep Fit Association does its best to ensure that its members bring themselves up to a good degree of athleticism and remain in good physical fettle. Ladies' Day at the Hall is always popular and entertaining even though there is hardly a man in sight, but perhaps men do not relish the idea of giving exhibitions with balls, clubs, hoops, ribbons, ropes and scarves or of dancing and skipping.

The sports with the longest and most chequered history at the Hall are wrestling and boxing and both had to experience considerable opposition before they could break the ice of Edwardian conservatism and the inhibitions and impediments contained in the Hall's constitution. So far as wrestling was concerned these slight difficulties were overcome by the *Daily Chronicle*, promoter of the first bout on 2nd July 1904, using the subterfuge of presenting a Physical Culture Entertainment in the course of which the great Russian wrestler, Georges Hackenschmidt, defeated Tom Jenkins, champion of the United States, for the World Championship and a purse of £2,500. Prior to the event a Special Entertainment Committee comprising Lord Ilchester and Sir William Makins considered the application and received from two representatives of the newspaper "The assurance that the display would be entirely

Opposite: Hardly a man in sight as members of the Keep Fit Association give a display.

Right: A competitor in one of the gymnastics events held in the Royal Albert Hall.

C. Christodoulou

free from anything vulgar or incompatible with the dignity and reputation of the Royal Albert Hall, and that the Competitors would be properly clothed so that there would be nothing of the semi-nude in the Entertainment, and that steps would be taken to ensure absolute order and propriety''. The dignity and reputation of the Royal Albert Hall was guaranteed by the *Chronicle* engaging a military band, prohibiting boxing and betting, providing adequate Police supervision, including fencing and exhibition wrestling in the programme, ensuring that no violence was perpetrated by the competitors against each other and that the Championship bout would be a genuine contest. Having received all these assurances of decorous behaviour the Physical Culture Entertainment was permitted to take place and so create a precedent for future years. Wrestling is now a frequent and regular feature of activity at the Hall, contests being put on five or six times a year and it has become something of a wrestling Mecca since competitors from all over the world are eager to try their luck and demonstrate their expertise at the most famous and prestigious of venues. Most of the ''greats'' have appeared at one time or another and the general consensus seems to be that the sport, along with music, attracts the best behaved crowds.

On 22nd May 1963 the Duke of Edinburgh became the first member of the Royal Family in modern times to attend a wrestling contest, the last occasion it is believed being in early Tudor times. The International Tournament was in aid of the Duke's Award Scheme so that fact may have had much, if not all, to do with the presence of His Royal Highness, though he was present again on 11th

July 1968 at a promotion in aid of the St John Ambulance Brigade. The Duke of Kent has also been present on occasions.

Boxing had an even longer struggle than wrestling before it broke into the auspicious confines of the Royal Albert Hall. As early as 1893 a Mr B. Hyams of the *Railway Tavern*, Hackney, had his application to promote a tournament spread over six nights rejected by the Council with the succinct declaration that "The consensus of opinion being decided against the proposal, it was declined". The august Amateur Boxing Association fared no better when in January 1902 it applied to hold its Annual Championship Competitions in the Hall; this time the proposal was declined in even fewer words than before—simply "in accordance with precedent". In June of the same year the organisers of the Coronation Tournament held on the 14th of the month were instructed to delete boxing items from the event "in consequence of the King's disapproval of the introduction of professional pugilists into the Royal Albert Hall".

One of the contestants in the lightweight competition goes down during the Amateur Boxing Association's championship meeting in 1937. *B.B.C. Hulton Picture Library*

The first real break for the sport came six years later on 21st July 1908 when the Council pondered the question whether permission should be given for the Amateur Boxing Association's Annual Championships in the Autumn; what undoubtedly swayed the ultimate decision was that the event was in connection with the Olympic Games but even so permission was couched in restrained terms and hedged about with qualifications. The ultimate responsibility was laid on Edward VII's shoulders and perhaps the Council hoped, knowing his antipathy to pugilism, that he would gather any odium that might accrue from an unfavourable decision when the application was accepted "Subject to the approval of His Majesty the King, and to a satisfactory assurance being given by the Association that there would be nothing objectionable in the Competition, and that they would take every precaution to ensure the same". The King did approve and the promoters carried out their required obligations though it cost them £150 inclusive of expenses to hire the Hall for three hours.

Further inroads were made during the First World War when the Services Tournaments were held in the Hall though still there were restrictions imposed to the effect that "The contests will be strictly limited to soldiers and sailors of His Majesty's Forces, and that the Tournament will be under the direct auspices and control of the Army and Navy Boxing Association". Furthermore it was stated that the President of the Council had to be satisfied with the Committee of Management responsible for staging the event; the Council certainly liked to cover its tracks by leaving the ultimate decision to an individual—firstly the King and then its own President. When a Sports Display and Concert took place on 17th April 1915 in aid of the British Red Cross Society doubts and indecision about boxing and wrestling were suddenly laid to rest and permission seems to have been granted without demur, no doubt with the worthiness of the cause in mind. It is difficult to believe otherwise, particularly in view of all the fuss generated about the Services Tournaments, but whatever the reason the event must have been quite notable judging from the varied sporting activities other than boxing and wrestling, to say nothing of the concert. Sergeant Jim Driscoll and Bombadier Billy Wells boxed a few exhibition rounds and there was fencing (foils, epée, sabre and bayonet), ju-jitsu, feats of strength, including weight lifting by Britain's strongest man, and a gymnastic and physical exercises display by the Harrodian Ladies Gymnastic Club.

By now a foot was in the door which was then pushed half open in 1919 when, on Boxing Day of all days, the Hall was let for a series of a dozen events "with the approval of the President and as many members of the Council as were available during the vacation". For the first time all the limitations were lifted, George V actually presented a gold trophy for competition and it required little imagination to wonder what his father would have thought of such an act of generosity. The great Georges Carpentier fought three exhibition rounds but there was no financial return for him or the other participants, everything was on a strictly amateur basis but the barriers were going down fast, one more being knocked over on 13th January 1921 when the Prince of Wales occupied a ring-side seat and saw Pete Harman beat Jimmy Wilde in the 17th round. Since then the late Duke of Gloucester and Prince Charles have witnessed fights. 1925 was the year when the first contests were held for monetary awards and they brought trouble from the Police in their wake since repeated reports were circulating that betting on the bouts was being permitted. Constitutionally betting was not permitted on the premises so the Council had to get over the problem and put itself on the right side of the law by having announcements made from the ring that anyone found contravening the ban would be ejected from the Hall. That little problem solved others soon raised their heads with the popularity of the sport attracting the big names to perform, resulting in the box office doing record business; it also brought in its train a black market in tickets which changed hands at grossly inflated prices, even seat-holders being suspected of participating in the racket. At the time such a practice was quite legal on the premises but a by-law now prohibits such low cunning. On one occasion forged tickets made their appearance but were quickly traced after a group were discovered printed for a non-existent row. Then again boxing attracted certain undesirable elements, particularly in the inter-war years, and the decisions of referees were frequently challenged and led to some disorder, particularly in the form of booing and cat-calls; on such occasions the organ came in useful, the trouble-makers standing little chance against the mighty volume of the instrument. Even today the general opinion seems to affirm that boxing draws the roughest of all crowds to the Hall.

Boxing is now a commonplace event in the Hall, being promoted even more frequently than wrestling, and raises not so much as a flicker of an eyebrow by way of protest. Great names there have been and presumably will continue to be, ranging from the days of Primo Carnero, whose first fight in Britain was in the Hall, to Randolph Turpin, Chris Finnegan and Alan Minter. Several highly prestigious contests have taken place including the European Heavyweight Championship when Bugner beat Ros; the European Bantamweight Championship, won by Alan Rudkin; the World Welterweight Championship, when Emile Griffith beat Harry (Gt) Scott; the World Featherweight Championship when Winstone beat Saki, and the European Flyweight Championship when Charlie Magri beat Enrique Rodriguez Cal. Mohammed Ali boxed eight exhibition rounds on 9th October 1971. The Police Force Championships have also been held on several occasions. Closely allied to boxing and wrestling are judo and karate. The European Karate Championships were contested in 1971 and black-belt judo was introduced in 1958 and repeated in 1960 and 1968. The Oriental Art of Self Defence was demonstrated in April 1974 and on 9th March 1981 a team of Kung-Fu and Yinggigong experts from the People's Republic of China gave a Grand Display of the Martial Arts.

Within the limitations imposed by its shape and size the Hall has had a remarkable sporting record, the surprise omission perhaps being skating, both ice and roller. In the case of ice skating Charles Cochran, when he was Manager, installed a rink in the Basement but like some other sports it did not appeal. Perhaps nearly 60 years on another attempt might prove more successful!

Epilogue

IN CHAPTER One I have quoted words from the *Illustrated London News'* account of the foundation-stone laying ceremony and it is perhaps fitting to conclude this book with a further extract from the same report—"May future generations of Englishmen look back upon the commencement of this enterprise and couple the name of its Royal projector with feelings of profound veneration and unfeigned gratitude!" Now, at the end of 110 years of history, there is little doubt that this has been accomplished and will continue to be so in the years to come.

APPENDIX ONE

Verbatim Extracts from Queen Victoria's Journals, Royal Archives, Windsor Castle

The following are the Royal names referred to in the Journals:-
Louise—Princess Louise, Marchioness of Lorne, later Duchess of Argyll. **Leopold**—Prince Leopold, Duke of Albany. **Baby (Beatrice)**—Princess Beatrice, Princess Henry of Battenburg. **Christian**—Prince Christian of Schleswig-Holstein. **Lenchen**—Princess Helena, Princess Christian of Schleswig-Holstein. **Bertie**—Albert Edward, Prince of Wales, later King Edward VII. **Affie**—Prince Alfred, Duke of Edinburgh. **Arthur**—Prince Arthur, Duke of Connaught. **George C**—Duke of Cambridge. **Augusta Strelitz**—Princess Augusta of Cambridge, Grand Duchess of Mecklenburg-Strelitz. **Adolphus**—Adolphus, Hereditary Grand Duke of Mecklenburg-Strelitz. **Ernest Coburg**—Ernest II, Duke of Saxe-Coburg-Gotha. **Lorne**—Marquis of Lorne, later Duke of Argyll. **Alice**—Princess Alice, Grand Duchess of Hesse-Darmstadt. **Empress**—Augusta, German Empress, wife of William I, German Emperor. **Louischen**—Princess Louise of Prussia, Duchess of Connaught. **Helen**—Princess Helen of Waldeck and Pyrmont, Duchess of Albany. **Victoria S.H.**—Princess Helena Victoria of Schleswig-Holstein.

20 May 1867

A muggy day—At ½ p 10 started for London, with Louise, Leopold, Baby and all the Ladies and Gentlemen (the latter, in uniform). Christian met us at the station, as well as Lenchen, but she did not accompany me. A little rain been falling, the sky was heavy and the air oppressive, but by the time we reached Paddington it cleared and was quite fair. Got into open carriages, of which there were 6, & 4 horses, with Ascot liveries, & had a full Escort of the Life Guards with standard and trumpeter. Great crowds everywhere & much enthusiasm. We drove through the Park over the bridge, down Rotten Row and down the Albert Road up to the place adjoining the Horticultural, where the Hall is to be. It was enclosed & covered in by an enormous tent. Here I got out being received by Bertie with an enormous white bouquet, brought from Paris (he having only arrived this morning)—Affie and Arthur with the other members of the Committee and was conducted to the place where the stone was to be laid. On the platform erected for me stood George C., Augusta Strelitz & Adolphus. The place was full of people, about 6000 or more, numbers of whom I knew. The National Anthem was sung and then came that most trying moment, from which I suffered severely,—the reading of the Address by Bertie, & my answer, both full of allusions to my beloved, which agitated me dreadfully, & I was nearly overcome, though I managed to command myself. This over, I went down to the lower platform, only accompanied by our children and those engaged in the laying of the stone. The usual ceremony was gone through, the Arch-bishop of Canterbury offering up a short prayer. What was very moving and again nearly upset me, was the flourish of trumpets, whilst the stone slowly descended into its place. I then returned to my former place and dearest Albert's composition, the "Invocazione all'Armonia" was performed under the direction of Costa. Mario's voice, which my beloved one so admired, sang his solo beautifully though he is now 61! How I thought of dearest Albert's feeling so shy about ever having this composition performed, which I had helped in writing down for him, and in singing the solos for him. The National Anthem was again sung and accompanied by our children, preceded by all our Gentlemen and followed by the Ladies and persons connected with the Horticultural Socy, I walked through the immense assemblage to the door of the Conservatory, where I was received by the Duke of Buccleuch and others, who showed us some fine flowers. I was taken by the north western terrace of the garden (full of people) to my carriage. Drove in the same way down Rotten Row and then Constitution Hill, all full of cheering crowds, but only my carriage went on to Marlborough House.

December 3, 1870

Dull and very cold—shortly before 10, left for London with Beatrice, the Dss. of Roxburghe & the 2 Equerries and drove straight to the Albert Hall, where we got out. It is greatly improved in appearance since it is nearly finished and the frieze and work outside is very handsome. The inside of the building (the structural part) is finished, the decorations having only just been started and there is much scaffolding still up. A lady sang and a violinist played, to test the effect of sound, which was extremely good. We walked a little way round the Galleries and upstairs. It certainly is a splendid building & I hope & trust may pay. How much it made me think of good Gen. Gray whose whole heart was in it, and who always feared he would not live to see the building completed. The Memorial looks beautiful without the scaffolding. From here we drove to Argyll Lodge.

March 25, 1871

After luncheon saw Sir M Costa about the opening of the Albert Hall.

March 29, 1871

Very dull and very raw and cold. Ernest C, Arthur and Beatrice breakfasted with me. At a little after 12, started in 9 dress closed carriages (mine with a pair of creams) for the Albert Hall, for its opening. I drove with dear Alice and Ernest Coburg. Lenchen, Louise, Beatrice and Arthur in the next carriage, Leopold, Christian & Lorne following & then the suites. Immense & very loyal crowds. Bertie received us at the door and then we walked up the centre of the immensely crowded Hall (8,000 people were there) which made me feel quite giddy. Bertie read the address from the dais, to which he had been conducted, very well and I handed to him the answer saying ''In handing you this answer I with to express my great admiration of this beautiful Hall and my earnest wishes for its complete success''. This was greatly applauded. The National Anthem was sung after which Bertie declared the Hall open. Good Mr Cole was quite crying with emotion and delight. It is to Col. Scott of the Engineers, who built the Hall, that the success of the whole is due. We then went upstairs to my box, which is not quite in the centre, and heard Costa's Cantata performed, which is very fine. I had never been at such a big function since beloved Albert's time, and it was naturally trying & ''émotionnant'' for me. I thought of poor dear Gen. Grey who had been so enthusiastic and anxious about this undertaking and who was not permitted to see the building completed. It was opened 2 days before the 1st anniversary of his death. Lenchen and Louise returned with me, the others remaining for the concert which followed.

May 8, 1872 Windsor Castle.

The same dreadful weather . . . At ¼ p 4 left in 5 closed carriages for the Albert Hall, the Equerries riding. The Empress, Lenchen & Beatrice drove with me. The 3 Princes* received me at the Hall. We went up at once to the Royal Box & were extremely well received. Remained for the first part of the Grand Choral Concert, conducted by Gounod. His Te Deum is extremely fine, as are all his compositions. The Chorus & Choir were all amateurs. As we were going out the Dss. of Buccleuch presented young Ld. Aberdeen, a nice looking young man.

February 25, 1876

At ¼ to 4 went with Beatrice, Leopold and the suite to a concert at the Albert Hall, where I was received by Affie & 2 of the principal people. The Hall was very full and there were great crowds outside. We went in Town Coaches the Equerries riding. The Concert was excellent. Albani's singing of the well known Aria from the ''Puritani'', which I had not heard for years, was quite beautiful, every note, even the softest could be heard with perfect distinctness. The selections of Russian sacred music (choral) very fine. We stopped till after a solo on the organ and got back at ¼ to 6.

*Duke of Edinburgh, Prince Arthur and Prince Christian.

February 26, 1886

A beautiful day, 10 degrees of frost—out with Beatrice after breakfast—had an early luncheon and left for London. Went to the Albert Hall where Lenchen, Arthur, Louischen and Louise met us. The Hall was completely full, over 7,000 people, who cheered me most enthusiastically. Gounod's "Mors et Vita", somewhat shortened, was given. It was really splendid. Albani, Santley and Mme Patey sang beautifully. I was again immensely cheered when I left. Got back before dinner.

May 8, 1888 Buckingham Palace.

At ½ p 3 went to the Albert Hall, with Lenchen, Helen & Victoria S.H., Louise & Christian meeting me there, where Sullivan's "Golden Legend" was most beautifully given. The Hall was very full & it was very hot. The Choir of the Royal Albert Hall Choral Society sang the choruses. Albani sang exquisitely & the music is lovely. There was a pause between the parts & at the conclusion, before I left, I spoke to Albani, Mme Patey, Dr. Stainer, who presided at the organ, Mr Watkin Mills, Mr Banks, Mr Henschel & lastly Sir A. Sullivan, whom I complimented very much There was a great crowd outside, who cheered very much.

These passages from Queen Victoria's Journal are published by gracious permission of Her Majesty the Queen.

APPENDIX TWO

Royal Addresses and The Bishop of London's Prayer at the Opening of the Royal Albert Hall on 29 March 1871

Prince of Wales' Address

May it please your Majesty,—As President of the Provisional Committee of the Royal Albert Hall of Arts and Sciences, it is my high privilege and gratification to report to your Majesty the successful completion of this Hall, an important feature of a long-cherished design of my beloved father, for the general culture of your people, in whose improvement he was always deeply interested. Encouraged by your Majesty's sympathies, and liberally supported by your subjects, we have been enabled to carry out the work without any aid from funds derived from public taxation. I am warranted in expressing our confidence that this building will justify the conviction we expressed in the report submitted on the occasion of your Majesty's laying its first stone, that by its erection we should be meeting a great public want. Your Majesty's Commissioners for the Exhibition of 1851 in further prosecution of my father's design for the encouragement of the Arts and Sciences, an object which he always had warmly at heart, are about to commence a series of annual international exhibitions, to the success of which this Hall will greatly contribute by the facilities which it will afford for the display of objects and for the meeting of bodies interested in the industries which will form the subjects of successive exhibitions. The interest shown in the Hall by the most eminent musicians and composers of Europe strengthens our belief that it will largely conduce to the revival among all classes of the nation of a taste for the cultivation of music. Your Majesty will hear with satisfaction that results have justified the original estimate of the cost of the building, and that, aided by the liberal assistance of your Exhibition Commissioners, the corporation will commence its management unfettered by pecuniary liabilities, and under conditions eminently calculated to ensure success. It is my grateful duty to return to your Majesty our humble thanks for the additional mark of your Royal favour which is conferred upon us by your auspicious presence on the present occasion, when our labours as a Provisional Committee are drawing to a close. We venture to hope that when we shall have resigned our functions into the hands of the governing body, which will be elected under the provisions of the Royal Charter granted to us, your Majesty will continue to the Corporation that measure of support which has been always graciously given to us.

Queen Victoria's Reply

I thank you for the loyal address which, as President of the Provisional Committee of the Hall of Arts and Sciences, you have presented to me. In opening this spacious and noble Hall, it gives me pleasure to acknowledge the generous spirit which has been manifested in the completion, by voluntary effort, of a work promising so much public usefulness. I cordially concur in the hope you have expressed, that this Hall, forming as it does part of a plan in which I must ever take a deep and personal interest, may largely, and permanently, contribute to the promotion, among my people, of the love of Arts, as well as to the success of the annual exhibitions, which will bring successively into instructive competition the choicest products of the industries of all nations. These objects could not fail to commend themselves at all times and all places to my sympathy and interest, fraught as they are with recollections of him to whose memory this Hall is dedicated, and whose dearest aim was to inspire my people with a love of all that is good and noble, and by closer knowledge and juster appreciation of each other to cultivate a spirit of goodwill and concord among the inhabitants of all regions., I gladly give the assurance of my support to the Corporation to which the Hall is about to be entrusted, and I earnestly hope that their efforts to promote the objects for which it has been constructed may be rewarded by a career of abiding success.

The Bishop of London's Prayer

Almighty and most merciful God, under whose protecting care this work, begun in Thy Holy Name, has been brought to its completion, fulfil and perfect, we beseech Thee, the designs of those who have erected this fabric for Thy honour and glory and for the moral and intellectual culture of Thy people. Grant that within these walls may ever be sought and found the knowledge which humbles while it elevates, the tastes which purify while they adorn, and only those true pleasures which are unsullied by the stain of evil. Sanctify human science by the grace of heaven; imbue the creations of art with the "beauty of holiness"; and make each step in the discovery of truth a nearer approach to Thee who art the Truth itself. Give peace in our time, O Lord; and knit the hearts of all together in loyalty, unity and Christian brotherhood, for Jesus Christ's sake. Amen.

APPENDIX THREE

Presidents of the Council

H.R.H. Prince of Wales, K.G.	1872-1888
H.R.H. The Duke of Edinburgh, K.G.	1888-1900
Earl Pembroke & Montgomery, G.C.V.O.	1901-1913
Earl Howe, G.C.V.O.	1913-1929
Rt. Hon. Sir William Bull, Bart	1929-1931
Earl of Onslow, G.B.E.	1931-1942
Earl of Lucan, G.C.V.O., K.B.E., C.B.	1942-1949
Sir John Wardlaw-Milne, K.B.E.	1949-1952
The Lord Pender, C.B.E.	1952-1965
Sir Louis Gluckstein, G.B.E., T.D., Q.C.	1965-1979
Sir Kirby Laing, M.A., F.Eng., J.P., D.L.	1979-

APPENDIX FOUR

The Frieze

The following is based on a contemporary description of the frieze traversing the building in an anti-clockwise direction.

Over the porch is an allegorical composition by E. J. Poynter, A.R.A., representing the various countries of the world bringing in their offerings to the Exhibition of 1851. Britannia, throned under a species of canopy, has on either side female figures typical of peace and concord, and beyond them, again, others emblematical of plenty and prosperity. The slumbering lions which guard the throne are reined and played with by Cupids, and at the foot of the throne winged figures with trumpets summon all nations to the great world's show. From the left are approaching the Continents of Europe and America, and from the right come Asia and Africa; all of them characterised by female figures with armorini bearing before them banners inscribed with their names. America, with a mural crown, leads up a negro, whose fetters have been struck off, laden with a bale of cotton, and behind them comes an Indian chief bearing on high his calumet, in token of peace. Next the throne is Europe, attended by figures emblematical of Philosophy and Mechanical Invention, while in their train is a mechanic with his tool-basket, and a husbandman bearing grapes. Opposite them, following Asia are two gorgeously-dressed Asiatics, with men bearing a tea-chest, and saluting after the Indian fashion. The figure of Africa is, perhaps, one of the most successful and characteristic in the entire frieze—a negro princess, under the shade of her umbrella, followed by a Bedouin and a native bearing tusks of ivory.

Following on the right of Poynter's work is a series of three sections by F. R. Pickersgill, R.A., representing ''Music'', ''Sculpture'', and ''Painting''. A harpist typifies the early state of the art, when the musician wandered from castle to castle, ever welcome and entertained for his art's sake. The lady, the baron, and the knight, are listening to him with rapt attention. Then a merry bridal procession, preceded by musicians leading to the dance. Lastly, the lover and his mistress, indicating the other great incentive to music and poetry, the great passion, love.

In ''Sculpture'', we have a youth carving a crucifixion watched by a group of maidens, who appear to feel intensely the agony of the scene he has placed before them. Next, a mason carving a font, and some monks at work at a recessed wall-tomb, while one of them tries the effect of natural foliage in the spandrils as a suggestion for the decoration.

Nicola Pisano shows the drawings for his beautiful pulpit at Pisa to his friends, and Benvenuto Cellini holds aloft the famous cup or tazza associated with his name; while Michelangelo, pausing from work, gazes at his friend's chef d'oeuvre. The last subject of this group is ''Painting''. First a monkish missal painter, illuminating the parchment MSS. Then the painter showing his altar-piece or triptych to the delighted cardinal, with attendants bearing his Bible and purse. After him we see the worker in enamels heating his colours to melt them before applying them to a metal lectern by his side. Then some girls with flowers and fruit, suggesting a subject to some artists who are watching them; and lastly, a mother and child sitting to Raphael for one of his beautiful pictures of the Madonna. The whole of Pickersgill's work is executed with a firm graceful outline, and an absence of internal lines in the figure proves that he has studied the nature of the material he was designing for.

Over the Western porch is a subject by E. Armitage, A.R.A., entitled ''Princes, Art Patrons and Artists''. In the centre is the Parthenon, and around it are grouped princes and royal personages in consultation; on the extreme left of the composition the painter of an Etruscan vase is exhibiting his handiwork to some patrons, and an artist is showing his masterpiece to two warriors. On the right of the central group a sculptor unveils a recumbent lion, in order to show it to his visitors; a slave draws off the drapery which covers it.

The three following sections are all from the designs of W. F. Yeames, A.R.A.—"Workers in Stone", "Workers in Wood and Brick", and "Architecture". As an illustration of working in stone is the carving of one of the Metopes of the Parthenon, some war between the Centaurs and "The godlike kings of old". Then we have the dedication of a Greek temple, a priest offering sacrifice. Next some Roman edifice in process of erection, masons at work placing the stones in position; and a triumphant warrior returning victorious under the arch erected to commemorate some former conquest; the art of mosaic-working is shown by a man engaged in the mosaic inlay of some twisted column, such as those to be found in the cloisters of St John Lateran at Rome.

The art of brickmaking takes us back many centuries further in the world's history than masonry—the first building of which we possess any record, the Tower of Babel, was a brick structure. Yeames, however, shows us the Israelites at work in Egypt under their hard taskmasters, tempering the clay, moulding the bricks, and drying them in the sun. Next they toil at the removal of some ponderous sphinx, conveying it to its position in the approach to a temple guarded by twin obelisks, as at Luxor. As wood-workers, a man felling a tree, others raising into its place the wooden column of an ancient temple, and finally, some such early wooden structure as is thought to have suggested the origin of the Greek styles, which we now call the five orders of architecture.

In his third section, Yeames gives a brief summary of the art of architecture in Christian times. Here is the dedication of the Cathedral of St Sophia by the Emperor Constantine; a king or emperor considering the plans for a cathedral which an architect is submitting to him; masons and labourers transporting stone, and passing before a wayside cross. Next the West front of Peterborough Cathedral, and a group of workmen engaged in the construction of some renaissance building. This section of the frieze is terminated by a view of St Paul's Cathedral, in front of which are King Charles the Second and Sir Christopher Wren.

On the southern end of the hall another group of figures from the designs of Pickersgill, representing "The Infancy of the Arts and Sciences".

The three following portions of the frieze were designed by H. S. Marks, A.R.A. His first subject is "Agriculture"—a man ploughing with a yoke of oxen; the sower, the reaper, girls binding up the sheaves and bearing them away on their heads, typical of the ingathering into barns. A group of shepherds with their sheep and dogs shows the other great branch of rural industry. The next subject is "Horticulture and Land Surveying"—men and maidens working in a garden, planting and watering the flowers; pruning fruit trees and gathering the ripened fruit; vine dressing and girls with grapes; then some men measuring from an ancient terminal figure or boundary mark, and a Roman architect or engineer inspecting the plans of a tower or citadel held before him by an assistant; lastly some General or Emperor receiving the chart of a conquered country, while his soldiers lead before him some captives in heavy chains, natives of the country they have subdued.

The third subject by Marks is "Astronomy and Navigation"—shepherds keeping watch over their flocks by night, perhaps Chaldean astrologers, studying the stars; a Greek philosopher and his pupil. Then the discoverer of the telescope and its secrets, Galileo, with some students of astronomy; and to form a division of the subject, a transit instrument telling us of modern scientific discoveries. Navigation is shown by a man hollowing out a rude boat; then the seaman guiding his course by a star; and lastly we see a quaint ship of the Tudor time. A lighthouse ends the subject, to remind us of the progress made in the art of navigation since the time when men could only creep round the coast in daylight for want of landmarks in the dark by which to steer their frail craft.

Over the Eastern Entrance Porch is another design by Armitage, "A Group of Philosophers, Sages and Students". In the centre is a chair of honour, on which is seated the Chief Philosopher of the School, at his feet are female figures distributing rewards.

The next section is from the designs of J. C. Horsley, R.A.—the subject being "Engineering". Firstly, labourers quarrying the iron ore; then a smelting furnace just being tapped to withdraw its fiery charge; next a rolling-mill for converting the puddled iron into sheets and bars—the processes for converting the raw material into articles for the engineer's use. As results of his science, we have the electric telegraph and the locomotive engine; while a group of sappers engaged on a survey illustrates another branch of the subject.

Armstead has dealt with "The Mechanical Powers". At one end of his design is Archimedes, as the father of all engineering work, while James Watt is justly selected as the representative of modern achievements. Nude figures moving a block of stone, driving home a wedge, and working a wine-press give us examples of the applications of the various powers.

With Pickersgill's design for "Pottery and Glass-Making" the circuit is complete.

APPENDIX FIVE

Organ Specification

The organ was built by Henry Willis in 1871-72. It was rebuilt by Harrison and Harrison, the main part in 1924 and the remainder in 1933.

A programme of restoration was undertaken from 1954 onwards, and the pitch was raised. In 1972-73, the coupler and combination actions were converted to a solid-state system; the console was provided with a new piston layout; the Great Organ was made playable in two divisions; and some alterations were made to the unenclosed Choir Division.

PEDAL ORGAN, 36 Stops, 4 *Couplers*

No.	Stop			Pitch
1.	Acoustic Bass	(from 7)		64
2.	Double Open Wood	(from 7)		32
3.	Double Open Diapason	(from 9)		32
4.	Contra Violone	(from 64)		32
5.	Double Quint	(from 9)		21$\frac{1}{3}$
6.	Open Wood I			16
7.	Open Wood II			16
8.	Open Diapason I			16
9.	Open Diapason II			16
10.	Violone			16
11.	Sub Bass			16
12.	Salicional			16
13.	Viole	(from 48)	in Choir Box	16
14.	Quint			10$\frac{2}{3}$
15.	Octave Wood	(from 6)		8
16.	Principal	(from 8)		8
17.	Violoncello			8
18.	Flute			8
19.	Octave Quint			5$\frac{1}{3}$
20.	Super Octave			4
21.	Harmonics	10, 12, 15, 17, 19, 21, 22		VII
22.	Mixture	15, 19, 22, 26, 29	in Solo box	V
23.	Double Ophicleide	(from 25)		32
24.	Double Trombone	(from 27)	in Swell box	32
25.	Ophicleide			16
26.	Bombard			16
27.	Trombone		in Swell box	16
28.	Fagotto			16
29.	Trumpet	(from 115)	in Swell box	16
30.	Clarinet	(from 60)	in Choir box	16
31.	Bassoon	(from 129)	in Solo box	16
32.	Quint Trombone			10$\frac{2}{3}$
33.	Posaune	(from 25)		8
34.	Clarion			8
35.	Octave Posaune	(from 25)		4
36.	Bass Drum			

I. Choir to Pedal
II. Great to Pedal
III. Swell to Pedal
IV. Solo to Pedal

CHOIR AND ORCHESTRAL ORGAN,
27 Stops, *Tremulant,* 5 *Couplers and* 1 *Transfer*

First Division (Choir), *unenclosed,*
11 Stops *and* 1 *Transfer*

No.	Stop		Pitch
37.	Open Diapason		8
38.	Lieblich Gedeckt		8
39.	Dulciana		8
40.	Gemshorn		4
41.	Lieblich Flute		4
42.	Nazard		2$\frac{2}{3}$
43.	Flageolet		2
44.	Tierce		1$\frac{3}{5}$
45.	Mixture	15, 19, 22	III
46.	Trumpet		8
47.	Clarion		4

V. Choir (unenclosed) on Solo

Second Division (Orchestral), *enclosed,*
16 Stops, *Tremulant and* 3 *Couplers*

No.	Stop		Pitch
48.	Contra Viole		16
49.	Violoncello		8
50.	Viole d'Orchestre I		8
51.	Viole d'Orchestre II		8
52.	Viole Sourdine		8
53.	Violes Celestes	2 ranks	8
54.	Viole Octaviante		4
55.	Cornet de Violes	12, 15, 17, 19, 22	V

VI. Tremulant

56. Quintaton 16
57. Harmonic Flute 8
58. Concert Flute 4
59. Harmonic Piccolo 2
60. Double Clarinet 16
61. Clarinet 8
62. Orchestral Hautboy 8
63. Cor Anglais 8

VII. Octave
VIII. Sub Octave
IX. Unison off } *(Second Division only)*

X. Swell to Choir
XI. Solo to Choir

GREAT ORGAN, 31 Stops, 3 *Couplers and* 2 *Transfers*

First Division, 21 Stops *and* 1 *Transfer*

64. Contra Violone 32
65. Contra Gamba 16
66. Double Claribel Flute 16
67. Open Diapason I 8
68. Open Diapason III 8
69. Open Diapason IV 8
70. Viola da Gamba 8
71. Rohr Flute 8
72. Quint ... ... $5\frac{1}{3}$
73. Principal 4
74. Viola 4
75. Harmonic Flute 4
76. Octave Quint ... ... $2\frac{2}{3}$
77. Super Octave 2
78. Harmonics ... 10, 15, 17, 19, 21, 22 ... VI
79. Contra Tromba 16
80. Tromba 8
81. Octave Tromba 4
82. Posaune 8
83. Harmonic Trumpet 8
84. Harmonic Clarion 4

XII. Reeds on Choir

Second Division, 10 Stops *and* 1 *Transfer*

85. Double Open Diapason 16
86. Bourdon 16
87. Open Diapason II 8
88. Open Diapason V 8
89. Geigen 8
90. Hohl Flute 8
91. Octave 4
92. Fifteenth 2
93. Mixture ... ... 8, 12, 15, 19, 22 ... V
94. Cymbale ... ... 19, 22, 26, 29, 31, 33, 36 VII

XIII. Great Second Division on Choir
XIV. Choir to Great
XV. Swell to Great
XVI. Solo to Great

SWELL ORGAN, 25 Stops, *Tremulant and* 3 *Couplers*

95. Double Open Diapason 16
96. Bourdon 16
97. Open Diapason 8
98. Viola da Gamba 8
99. Salicional 8
100. Vox Angelica 8
101. Flûte à Cheminée 8
102. Claribel Flute 8
103. Principal 4
104. Viola 4
105. Harmonic Flute 4
106. Octave Quint ... ... $2\frac{2}{3}$
107. Super Octave 2
108. Harmonic Piccolo 2
109. Mixture ... ... 8, 12, 15, 19, 22 ... V
110. Furniture ... 15, 19, 22, 26, 29 ... V
111. Contra Oboe 16
112. Oboe 8
113. Baryton 16
114. Vox Humana 8

XVII. Tremulant

115. Double Trumpet 16
116. Trumpet 8
117. Clarion 4
118. Tuba 8
119. Tuba Clarion 4

XVIII. Octave
XIX. Sub Octave
XX. Solo to Swell

SOLO AND BOMBARD ORGAN,
27 Stops, *Tremulant,* 6 *Couplers and* 2 *Transfers*

First Division (solo), *enclosed,*
17 Stops, *Tremulant and* 3 *Couplers*

120. Contra Brass 16
121. Flûte à Pavillon 8
122. Viole d'Amour 8
123. Doppel Flute 8
124. Harmonic Claribel Flute 8
125. Unda Maris ... 2 ranks 8
126. Wald Flute 4
127. Flauto Traverso 4
128. Piccola Traverso 2

XXI. Tremulant

129.	Double Bassoon	16
130.	Corno di Bassetto	8
131.	Hautboy	8
132.	Bassoon	8
133.	Double Horn	16
134.	French Horn	8
135.	Carillons (Tenor C)	
136.	Tubular Bells (Middle C)	

XXII. Octave
XXIII. Sub Octave
XXIV. Unison off

Second Division (Bombard),
10 Stops, 3 *Couplers and* 2 *Transfers*
137-143 *enclosed in Solo box*

137.	Bombardon		16
138.	Tuba		8
139.	Orchestral Trumpet		8
140.	Cornopean		8
141.	Quint Trumpet		5⅓
142.	Orchestral Clarion		4
143.	Sesquialtera	12, 15, 17, 19, 22	V

XXV. Octave
XXVI. Sub Octave
XXVII. Unison off

144.	Contra Tuba	16
145.	Tuba Mirabilis	8
146.	Tuba Clarion	4

XXVIII. Tubas on Choir
XXIX .Bombard on Choir

COMBINATION COUPLERS

XXX. Great and Pedal Combinations coupled
XXXI. Pedal to Swell Pistons

ACCESSORIES

9 adjustable foot pistons to Pedal Organ
9 adjustable pistons each to Great and Swell Organs
5 adjustable pistons each to Choir (unenclosed), Orchestral, and Solo Divisions
2 fixed pistons to Solo Division
5 fixed pistons to Bombard Division
12 adjustable general pistons (duplicated by foot pistons, which are also available by switch as Swell foot pistons)
Cancel piston to each manual
Pedal cancel foot piston
General cancel piston
Reversible pistons to I-IV, X, XI, XIV-XVI, XX and 25
Reversible foot pistons to II, IV and XVI
General crescendo pedal, with indicator

The combinations are instantly adjustable by setter.
The action is electro-pneumatic: the coupler and combination actions are on a solid-state system.
The manual compass is CC to C, 61 notes: the pedal CCC to G, 32 notes.
The pitch is C = 523·3 (A = 440) at 65°F.
New blowing plant was installed by Messrs. Watkins & Watson in 1955-56. A total of 42 h.p. is used: wind pressures range from 3 to 30 inches. The humidifiers are also by Messrs. Watkins & Watson.

Bibliography

The Fleet; its River, Prison and Marriages, J. Ashton, Fisher Unwin, 1888.
The Proms, Leslie Ayre, Leslie Frewin, 1968.
Southern England and East Anglia, K. Baedeker, George Allen & Unwin, 1966.
Survey of London Vol. 38 Museums Area. South Kensington and Westminster, P. A. Bezodis, The Athlone Press, 1975.
From Where I Sit, Jack Brymer, Cassell, 1979.
Knightsbridge and Belgravia, E. Beresford Chancellor, Pitman Books, 1909.
The Pleasure Haunts of London, E. Beresford Chancellor, Constable, 1925.
The Royal Albert Hall, Ronald W. Clark, Hamish Hamilton, 1958.
London Rebuilt 1897-1927, H. P. Clunn, John Murray, 1927.
The Face of London, H. P. Clunn, Simpkin Marshall, 1882.
The Henry Wood Proms, D. Cox, B.B.C. Publications, 1980.
Dictionary of London: Facsimile of 1879 edition, Charles Dickens, H. Baker, 1973
Pleasures of London, M. Willson Disher, Robert Hale, 1950.
The Harrison Story, L. Elvin, L. Elvin, 1977.
The Golden Echo, David Garnett, Chatto & Windus, 1953.
A Short History of the Royal Albert Hall, London, John B. Geale, Royal Albert Hall, 1956.
An Encyclopaedia of London, W. Kent (Ed.), J. M. Dent & Sons, 1951.
A Wanderer in London, E. V. Lucas, Metheun, 1906.
The London Week-End Book, Francis Marshall, Seeley Service, 1953.
The London Scene, H. J. Massingham, Cobden Sanderson, 1933.
King's England: London North of the Thames, Arthur Mee, Hodder & Stoughton, 1972.
Conversations with Menuhin, Yehudi Menuhin, Macdonald & Jane's, 1979.
Victorian London, Priscilla Metcalf, Cassell, 1972.
London, H. V. Morton, Methuen, 1937.
Nairn's London, Ian Nairn, Penguin Books, 1966.
Orchestra in England, R. Nettl, Jonathan Cape, 1946.
Discovering Victorian London, G. Norton, Macdonald General Books, 1969.
The Proms, Ates. Orga, David & Charles, 1974.
Royal Albert Hall Compendiums, Old Bond Street, 1973-81.
Old Kew, Chiswick & Kensington, Lloyd Sanders, Methuen, 1910.
Life in Victorian London, L. C. B. Seaman, B. T. Batsford, 1973.
The Royal Albert Hall of Arts and Sciences, The Solicitors' Law Stationery Society, 1966.
London Past and Present, Wheatley & Cunningham, John Murray, 1891.
London's Old Buildings and where to Find Them, Jessie D. Wright, George Allen & Unwin, 1936.

Index

Illustrations in bold type